Life Management

Swami Amartyananda

𝒜dvaita Ashrama

(PUBLICATION DEPARTMENT)

5 DEHI ENTALLY ROAD · KOLKATA 700 014

Published by
Swami Bodhasarananda,
Adhyaksha, Advaita Ashrama
Mayavati, Champawat ,Uttarakhand, Himalayas
from its Publication Department, Kolkata
www.advaitaashrama.org
mail@advaitaashrama.org

© Advaita Ashrama, 2009
All Rights Reserved
First Edition, May 2005
Published by Ramakrishna Mission Ashrama, Patna
Second Edition, January 2009
Sixth Reprint, August 2012
10M6C

ISBN 978-81-7505-323-6

Printed in India at
Trio Process
Kolkata · 700 014

Publisher's Note to the Second Edition

It gives us great pleasure to present to readers this thoroughly revised edition of *Effective Life Management*. The book was first published by the Ramakrishna Mission Ashrama, Patna, in 2005 to commemorate the 150th birth anniversary of Sri Sarada Devi. The book was very popular and quickly sold out. The increasing demand for books on this subject shows that there is an urgent desire in people to find practical ways to make life more meaningful—both on the individual and the collective level. In this edition a new chapter, 'Developing Will-power to Achieve True Success', has been added. Furthermore, some editing has been done on the earlier text to make it more readable. We are thankful to all those who have helped us in bringing out this new edition. It is our hope that it will be well received by one and all.

The copyright of this book has been transferred to Advaita Ashrama. For giving us permission to publish this second edition, we express our sincere thanks to the Ramakrishna Mission Ashrama, Patna.

12 January 2009   PUBLISHER
Advaita Ashrama, Kolkata

Publisher's Note to the First Edition

Holy Mother Sri Sarada Devi was the ideal Indian woman. Her life was dedicated to manifesting the divine power of the Motherhood of God. She was silent testimony to the truth of the Hindu scriptures. Her divine husband moulded her life so that she became a 'spiritual dynamo', to bless humanity. The current of her spiritual energy is silently transforming the lives of ordinary people even in far off lands. Sri Ramakrishna told her, 'After my passing away, you will have to do many things... You will do much more than I have done.'

Innumerable people, who have experienced Holy Mother's spiritual power, have attested it. Her chief attendant Swami Saradananda, also the first Secretary of the Ramakrishna Math and Mission, avowed that he had never seen a mind that was so great as Mother's nor did he ever expect to see in his lifetime another person with such sharp intelligence and deep understanding of life and its problems.

What qualities did the Holy Mother possess to make her so great a person?

First, she was divinely commissioned by the prophet of the modern age (*Yugavatara*) Sri Ramakrishna Paramahamsa and she realized God in her own right. Her pure and simple mind was capable of grasping subtle truths and could see into the heart of all things.

Second, the Holy Mother knew the essential spirit of the holy books although she was not a pundit of the Holy Scriptures such as the Gita and the Upanishads. She intuitively knew how to apply these lofty principles that were earlier restricted to scholarly discussions. For instance, she stressed the importance of 'introspection' —the need to look within, in order to resolve spiritual and mental problems. This makes her a practical guide to youngsters, who want to overcome negative feelings such as anger, obsessive desire and jealousy.

How should we manage the enemies lurking within our own mind, so that we can enjoy a peaceful and prosperous life? The way, Holy Mother emphasized, lies first in realizing that these are natural human emotions that trouble everyone. But, she said that one can gain mastery over them by constantly restraining the mind from going astray. The sense organs—eyes, ears, the organs of taste, touch, and smell must be restrained from going out to enjoy their natural objects. Then, peace follows. Just as the Gita (3.7) says, 'He who restrains his senses with his mind and directs his organs of action to work, with no feeling of attachment—he is indeed superior.'

Holy Mother also stressed that one should always keep oneself busy with some useful work to prevent unwanted thoughts from conquering our mind. Anger, lust, and jealousy are the greatest enemies of spiritual life—'all-devouring and the cause of all sin', as the Gita says (3.37).

Sri Sarada Devi, as she herself revealed, is our real Mother, a mother who really feels for all her children. She is the universal Mother and she incarnated to manifest universal Motherhood. Everyone, including animals, birds, and other creatures belonged to her and received equal love and attention. She never forced ideas on others and never restricted anyone by force but would warn them of the consequences of their dangerous actions. She believed in the transformative power of love and always gave perfect freedom to all.

To those who could not practise self-control, she would grant freedom to enjoy life—even all its poisons, for she could see that there was no other way to educate them about what was right or wrong. A disciple once wanted to know if it was possible for all to get rid of their desires. Holy Mother's affectionate and intelligent reply was, 'How can they? If they could, then creation would come to an end. The world is going on because not all can be free of desires.' To such people her assuring answer would be, 'Why do you worry so much? Fulfil all your worldly desires; afterwards you will enjoy abiding peace with Sri Ramakrishna. He has created a new heaven for you.'

To her spiritual children, Holy Mother would say, 'These feelings of desire are in everybody, they will remain as long as the body remains. As far as possible, one should not bother about innocent desires that come and go in our mind daily.' As the Lord says in the Gita (2.14) 'Notions of heat and cold, of pain and pleasure, arise only from the contact of the senses with their objects. They come and go; they are impermanent. Endure them, O Bharata!' However, more dangerous desires such as lust and anger should be controlled so that they do not manifest in our dealings with others. Otherwise our relationship with others will sour and we will have to suffer.

Holy Mother always emphasized on 'being detached' from all fleeting emotions, so that they do not get overly important. Her instruction to the devotees always took into account their special needs. A disciple asked how he could get rid of insignificant desires that cropped up in his mind. Mother said, 'In your case, these are not real desires. They are only fancies that appear and disappear. The more they do so, the better for you.'

Along with the practice of non-attachment, Holy Mother would say, we should always exercise our God-given power of endurance, 'Sa, Sa, Sa!' (Three letters of the Bengali alphabet, which sound similar and mean to endure.) She used to say that the person who endures all the good and bad that happen in life and keeps his faith in God, would succeed in the end and get over all the problems of life with flying colours.

Holy Mother's message has immense meaning for the people of today, who find themselves in a state of permanent unhappiness and dissatisfaction in spite of rapid material progress. It is seen that people have become increasingly effective in managing their careers and social lives, but are equally ineffective in managing the most fundamental aspect of their lives—which is the ability to have peace of mind. Accordingly, this book intends to provide some guiding tips on how one's life may be managed effectively in the light of Holy Mother's teachings.

I pray to Sri Ramakrishna, Holy Mother Sri Sarada Devi and Swami Vivekananda to bless us all and guide us towards a life of fulfilment and joy.

May 2005   Swami Tadgatananda
                                                    Secretary
                                  Ramakrishna Mission Ashrama
                                      Ramakrishna Avenue, Patna

Author's Note

People today put in a lot of effort and take great pains to learn the art of managing their prospective careers and professions by enrolling themselves in schools, colleges, universities, and professional organizations. What they do not realize is that curricular education does not give them all the education that life demands. They also need to learn 'Effective Life Management' or the art of managing their personal lives. Otherwise, they are bound to end up like most 'successful' people today—brilliant in their respective businesses but unsuccessful in building up happy, fulfilling lives.

No man can hope to achieve material progress exclusively, by depriving others. One can only progress as a part of the society he lives in—through interaction, cooperation and teamwork. Society is an organization, a coming together of individuals. The society that has achieved a harmonious understanding amidst its members, progresses faster and is more stable. It is needless to say that such a situation calls for and depends on the character of each individual in that society. Such a healthy society also helps in moulding the character of its youngsters, thereby achieving a general standard of welfare and well-being.

With the aim of helping individuals develop right values and habits, this book exhorts its readers to imbibe right thoughts. This culture can be acquired by following these three techniques:

1. *Satsanga*, which includes study of good literature, holy company and listening to uplifting music like *bhajans* and so on.

2. *Discipline*, which involves performing one's daily activities efficiently, in an organised and scheduled manner, and

3. *Meditation*, which is the process of watching the thought-flow of one's own mind with a view to gain control over one's emotions. This is to be practised at least for ten minutes every morning and evening.

The technique of watching the thought-flow is explained in greater detail in the Appendix. The language used in this book is direct. Day-to-day examples as well as illustrations using stories bring home the central theme of SDM—*Satsanga*, Discipline and Meditation.

The concept of SDM and the contents of the present book are based on Practical Vedanta as exemplified in the life and teachings of Sri Sarada Devi, the consort of Sri Ramakrishna and popularly known as the Holy Mother. The universal teachings of Vedanta are not the exclusive property of any particular sect or creed as they encompass everyone, irrespective of caste, colour, nationality, sex, race or religion. Vedanta—the end or the culmination of the Vedas holds a universal message and is meant for the betterment of all. This book encourages its readers to be faithful to their respective beliefs and cultivate the habit of SDM.

The idea of publishing a book on this subject evolved from the repeated persuasions and growing demand of sincere and well-meaning young people interacting with me during the weekend lecture programmes on 'Youth Development', which were being conducted by me earlier at the Ramakrishna Math and Mission centres in New Delhi and Lucknow. I am now continuing the programme at the Mumbai Ramakrishna Math and Mission centre as well.

To facilitate assimilation of concepts by the reader, the first chapter introduces the importance of Effective Life Management, Vedanta, Swami Vivekananda's advocacy of Practical Vedanta in our day-to-day lives and an easy way to achieve purification of the mind.

The second chapter presents the Holy Mother as the embodiment of Practical Vedanta.

The rest of the book is divided into two parts—The Essence of Life Management and Conflict Management. While the first part contains practical tips to guide us towards Effective Life Management, the second part focuses on tips to help us deal with various conflicts that arise in our daily lives.

The practice of SDM is dealt with in the Appendix, to help readers recollect the essence of this book. The readers, I hope will find enough and convincing reasons presented in the book to earnestly follow SDM in their own lives.

I am thankful to all those who have helped me in writing this book. I very much appreciate the keen interest with which Mr. Tushar Sinha and Mr. Vinod Taneja, my students, prepared this book.

Finally, I dedicate this book to my Guru, Srimat Swami Vireswaranandaji Maharaj.

Ramakrishna Math   Swami Amartyananda
12th Road, Khar
Mumbai 400052

Contents

1
Introduction

Importance of Effective Life Management

The technological developments of recent times have propelled the human race on a fast track of material progress. The dignified and leisurely pace of life is almost passé. People face tough competition to excel at every stage and in every sphere of worldly life. Our lives are marked by daily frustrating commutes to the work place and back, speedy means of travel, and instant communication using the latest gadgets. Urbanization is rapid and consumerism is rampant, as market driven economies are using novel ways to attract consumers. A blitzkrieg through the glamorous world of films, television, media, and sports pervades everywhere—in homes, on roads, doling out promises of instant gratification and overnight stardom.

Those who are capable of enjoying the fruits of material progress and facing the challenges of modern life are considered fortunate by society. But it is really a challenging task for those who are running this difficult race today. People are under constant stress to achieve social status and material prosperity. As a fallout, human relationships, family bonds, and value systems are strained. Demanding lifestyles translate into lesser physical exercise, irregular sleep patterns, and anxiety disorders, all resulting in various diseases. Stress and work pressure eat into our time and we end up spending less quality time with family, friends, and loved ones, resulting in broken relationships and superficial interactions. Pent up emotions and lack of creative and relaxing activities translate into erratic human behaviour and lack of compassion towards one another. People find it difficult to make even basic sacrifices and adjustments in life. Problems are further compounded by the usual human traits of greed, anger, jealousy, hatred, lust, and so on.

The purpose of stating all this is not to paint a bleak picture and conjure up an entirely grim scenario. Instead, the purpose is to help individuals identify their problems and remedy them by applying time-tested techniques that have been handed down over generations.

To understand how important it is to manage our lives effectively, we need to look at life in a holistic manner. Whether we are householders, monks, students, businessmen, servants, ministers or even 'nobodies'— we are all engaged in unceasing work, all through our lives, from birth to death. But most of us never pause to think, even once, why we do all this work.

Propelled by the insatiable material, emotional, and intellectual goals that modern social life demands, one naturally feels an urge to struggle for a better state of life than the present one. Each person tries, in his own way, to attain his cherished goals. Usually, one chooses his goal of life based on his psychological constitution and the environmental conditions in which he is placed. Changes in the goal may occur as one evolves physically, emotionally, and intellectually. Generally, man wants to achieve that which he thinks is within his reach. The question arises then, why does man aspire for a better state of life? It is because we all feel that upon attaining a higher state of life we will be happier, more at peace, freer, more powerful, and less miserable. We are somehow discontent with our present state of existence and want to get rid of anything that tends to limit us. In the heart of hearts every being craves for unalloyed happiness, uninterrupted peace. This is the inner quest of all humans and we are all trying best to attain it in our own ways, consciously or unconsciously. This search for peace, contentment and happiness is the underlying motive behind all our pursuits in life. From this it becomes obvious that we work incessantly only to attain contentment, happiness or bliss.

Some may admit that they work to obtain money or possessions or power, but a little bit of introspection will tell that these are only means to the real end—bliss. Animals too are struggling to attain bliss, but they are guided by instinct. They lack the intellect that we humans possess, the faculty that enables us to make decisions and discriminate right from wrong. Unfortunately, most humans function purely on the basis of instinct and make little or no use of their intellect.

The sages of India, since time immemorial, have applied their mind to find out the true nature of the individual. They have concluded that bliss is our real nature and that we are *amritasya putrah* (children of immortality). Whether we know it or not, we are constantly struggling to regain our true nature. In the process, errors and wrong decisions born of ignorance may lead us astray, but sooner or later, a time will come when we have to realize our true identity.

However, looking at the world around us, it appears that people are not bothered about attaining the kind of peace that we have discussed above. It is true that differences in individualities are shaped by what are called as *samskaras* (latent impressions on the mind). Therefore, each individual's approach and outlook will be different and we cannot set a general standard for all to adhere to. The common observation is that in spite of our ceaseless efforts, the peace and contentment that we desire, constantly eludes most of us. Even those who appear to be happy with the means to fulfil their desires are seen to suffer a lot, since they want more and more of what they have been handed on a platter. Then there are those who appear to be confused and lost and keep on blaming this or that for their failures. Some are able to achieve their desired goals after hard struggles, but the desired happiness still proves to be a chimera and a delusion for them.

If the end result brings unhappiness and frustration, all efforts appear meaningless. However this struggle is not completely worthless, as it is through this process that the individual gains experience and knowledge, thereby moving ahead towards his ultimate goal. It is like the shaping of an ornament from a piece of gold. The gold is to be heated and beaten to craft it into a valuable piece of art. Each mark or bend in the final artifact will have much effort invested in it and it is this effort that adds to the value and beauty of the ornament. Similarly, the various desires, actions, experiences, achievements, setbacks, and the knowledge that we gain as we live life, get uniquely reflected in our respective personalities, making us richer in wisdom and helping us develop emotional balance.

The extent to which we train our mind by strengthening our will-power and intellect will determine our personality. Our personalities can be said to be the outcome of our mind and its various reactions to external stimuli. A person is said to have an integrated personality when there is perfect conformity between his knowledge and actions. Such a person not only possesses wisdom, he also has the ability to conduct all his actions in a manner that reflects this inner wisdom. How one feels, eats, behaves—these and much more—shape an individual's personality.

The mind is very choosy. Usually, it dictates terms—it likes this, it does not like that. Using our intellect, we need to dictate it to follow the right course of action and avoid the wrong one. And we cannot direct our mind unless we control it. How then do we control our mind? Despite best efforts, our resolutions to control the mind gets weakened by gross and subtle desires and very often we get carried away by our drifting mind. We then feel weak and hopeless. How then should we strengthen and reform our character, to be able to develop a strong personality? How can we improve our will-power and develop confidence in our abilities? What concrete steps will help us attain our chosen goal of everlasting happiness, bliss, and peace? Here lies the importance of learning the art of managing one's personal life.

Vedanta: A Brief Introduction

Blessed indeed are we in India, to have inherited the accumulated knowledge in the form of spiritual truths which have been revealed from time to time in the hearts of men and women, purified by the practice of self-control and meditation. Such fortunate souls are called *rishis*, or seers of truth. *Rishi*-hood cannot be confined to a particular faith, caste, period, country or sex; quite a few of our *rishis* were women. They imparted their instructions in the crowded courts of kings, as well as in retreats beyond the bustle of the city. The super-sensuous experiences of these seers have been embodied in the Vedas. Twofold is the philosophy taught in the Vedas. One is the philosophy of *pravritti* or action and the other is the philosophy of *nivritti* or withdrawal from action, i.e. meditation. Both are required to establish a stable world order. Outward-going energy is *pravritti* and inward-going energy is *nivritti*. These energies are to be harmonized by the individual and the society, to ensure true material prosperity as well as spiritual growth and fulfilment for all beings. The Upanishads give us such verified and verifiable truths about human beings and the universe. The Upanishads are also known as Vedanta or the concluding chapters (*anta*) of the Vedas. The word 'Vedanta' literally means the end or goal of the Vedas, their essence. Vedanta, as a philosophy, is based on the Upanishads.

Practical Vedanta: Swami Vivekananda's Definition

Swami Vivekananda, during his extensive travels, came to the conclusion that in order to change man's condition for the better, religion must become a dynamic force in people's day-to-day lives. The sacred must permeate the secular. The Vedanta of the forest must be carried to the doors of every person, so that a teacher could be a better teacher; a student, a better student and a clerk, a better clerk.

Swami Vivekananda gave four lectures in London on Practical Vedanta in 1896 and one lecture in India on 'Vedanta in its Application to Indian Life' in Madras in 1897. In his first lecture on Practical Vedanta (The

Complete Works of Swami Vivekananda, vol.4, p.292), Swamiji says:

'In various Upanishads, we find that this Vedanta philosophy is not the outcome of meditation in the forests only, but that the very best parts of it were thought out and expressed by brains which were busiest in the everyday affairs of life.'

'Everything goes to show that this philosophy must be very practical; and later on, when we come to the Bhagavad Gita... curiously enough, the scene is laid on the battlefield, where Krishna teaches this philosophy to Arjuna; and the doctrine which stands out immensely in every page of the Gita is intense activity, but in the midst of it, eternal calmness. This is the secret of work, to attain which is the goal of Vedanta. Inactivity, as we understand it in the sense of passivity, certainly cannot be the goal... nor does inactivity become activity when it is combined with passion. Real activity, which is the goal of Vedanta, is combined with eternal calmness; the calmness, which cannot be ruffled, the balance of mind, which is never disturbed, whatever happens. And we all know from our experience in life that this is the best attitude for work.'

Speaking about the need to throw open the Upanishads to all human beings and the need to make the Upanishad teachings practical, Swamiji says:

'The Upanishads were in the hands of the *Sannyasin*; he went into the forest! Shankara was a little kind and said even *Grihasthas* (householders) may study the Upanishads, it will do them good; it will not hurt them. But still the idea is that the Upanishads talked only of the forest life of the recluse... the only commentary, the authoritative commentary on the Vedas, has been made once and for all by Him who inspired the Vedas—by Krishna in the Gita. It is there for every one in every occupation of life.' (*Complete Works*, Vol. 3, p.244)

Swami Vivekananda also upheld that the great truths realized by sages, ancient and modern, are not dogmas to be believed unquestioningly. They are meant to be realized and thereby verified. Truth is eternal and it already exists. But it is only when the mind is made absolutely pure and subtle that we achieve the concentration required to realize the subtlest of truths.

Everything depends on one's mind. Nothing can be achieved without purity of the mind. It is said, 'The aspirant may have received the grace of the Guru, the Lord, and the *Vaishnava*; but he comes to grief without the grace of the 'one'.' That 'one' is the mind. The mind of the aspirant should be gracious to him.

We need to know what is meant by purification of the mind and how to purify it. And more importantly, how do we manage our mind until it becomes absolutely pure and subtle?

Purification of the Mind: An Easy Way

The technique of managing our lives effectively, called SDM, contains 'S' which is an easy way to purify our mind. Every minute that we spend in *Satsanga*, which is the company of holy people, holy books, and so on, makes our mind that much stronger and purer. Even spending time in remembrance of the inspiring lives of holy people is included in the definition of *Satsanga*. When we reflect on the teachings of the great avatars and saints, our mind gets inspired and motivated to follow in their path, or at least, attachment to worldly things diminishes to some extent.

Each era has produced towering personalities like Rama, Krishna, Buddha, Moses, Jesus, Mohammed, Nanak, Ramakrishna and many others who elevated and changed the course of human development, so much so that each one of them is considered to be either a divine incarnation or God's messenger, by the faithful. Although they were normal human beings, they rose to the level of Gods and so; we can also aspire to be like them. Every great life has lessons galore for the teeming masses. It reveals the meaning and goal of life, and also shows us the right path. We look forward to be guided by their ideal conduct and teachings. The path shown by them may appear to be many, but the goal is only ONE—to lead us to contentment, happiness and bliss, or in other words to reveal to us, our true nature!

The life of a great person, whatever his area of specialization, always inspires. The incidents, small or big, in the lives of the great, serve as guidelines for others. Depending upon our temperament and the capacity to imbibe, we can learn lessons like love of God, love of man, modesty, simplicity, gentleness, forbearance, chastity, rationality, practicality and so on, from their lives. Swami Vivekananda says, 'As I grow older I look more and more for greatness in little things. I want to know what a great man eats and wears, and how he speaks to his servants...' When we read their lives we do find extraordinary greatness even in small day-to-day events.

And let us remind ourselves that we have set out to learn the art of effectively managing our lives with the aim of attaining happiness and peace through all our actions. In the second chapter that follows, the reader will be guided by the exemplary life of the Holy Mother, Sri Sarada Devi. A seemingly ordinary looking life was in fact a living example of the practical implementation of the precepts of Vedanta and is a source of inspiration to millions of people.

2
Meet Your Ideal: Sri Sarada Devi

In Sri Sarada Devi, the consort of Sri Ramakrishna, the world found a unique figure in its history. She combined in herself the roles of a perfect wife, nun, mother, teacher, and renunciate—all at the same time. Such a wonderful harmony of various ideals is rarely to be seen in the world. Simplicity, frugality, purity, and dignity were fully embodied in her form. Once she prayed to God, 'O Lord, there is a semblance of a black spot on the moon; let my life and character be more spotless, pure, clean, and calm than the moon.'

Sri Saradamani Devi, affectionately known to her devotees as the Holy Mother, was born in the village Jayrambati, West Bengal on 22, December 1853. Though her parents were poor in material matters, they possessed an inner wealth of steady faith in the grace of the Almighty. As was the common custom in those days, she was given in marriage to her husband, Sri Ramakrishna at the age of five. However it was not until much later in 1867, that she had the chance to live with him.

Sri Ramakrishna took upon himself the responsibility of training her in both worldly and spiritual matters. He imparted to her a thorough understanding of the human character and the life of complete resignation to God, which later helped her in spiritual ministrations. He awakened her inner divinity by worshipping her as the Divine Mother of the Universe and by proclaiming her unity with Mother Kali, who was worshipped in the temple. As her divinity unfolded, she expressed a sense of motherhood towards all creatures and that brought both saint and sinner to her feet.

The Holy Mother's life of austerity and simplicity, coupled with modesty and humility touches all those who come to learn about it. Unstintingly, she poured her blessings and wisdom to all those who approached her, without consideration of caste, creed or sex. As in her lifetime, even now, Mother continues to provide her devotees with solace and relief from the scorching cares of the world.

After Sri Ramakrishna entered *Mahasamadhi*, the Holy Mother guided the young disciples and householder devotees and thereby nurtured the roots of the Ramakrishna Order. She is therefore rightly considered as the *Sanghajanani*. The Holy Mother entered *Mahasamadhi* on 21, July 1920 in Kolkata.

Living amidst householders and catering to their incessant demands, she amply demonstrated through day-to-day interactions, the practical application and implementation of Vedanta philosophy. Her life proves

Swami Vivekananda's statement that Vedanta is not a subject to be pondered upon only in caves and monasteries, but that it is to be implemented in our everyday lives, and it should have an impact on even the most mundane of our activities.

Her life vindicates the fact that Vedanta can be practised by all; no matter how busy they are and how difficult their living conditions may be. She emphasized that every act must be done with care and due respect—whether it be the cutting of a wick for a lamp or the chopping of vegetables for cooking. She even reprimanded someone for throwing away a broom and insisted that it be kept away with due respect in its rightful place! To her, all work was equally important. She was a supreme example of Karma Yoga as taught by Swami Vivekananda in his lectures and by Lord Krishna in the battlefield of Kurukshetra.

During her final illness, the Holy Mother gave an advice, a supreme statement of the universality of spirit, human understanding, and oneness of soul to one of her devotees. She said, 'If you want peace of mind, don't find fault with others, but find fault rather with yourself. Learn to make the whole world your own. No one is a stranger, my dear; the whole world is your own.'

If we ponder over this apparently simple and beautiful message, we find that it conveys two essential truths of human life: the goal of human life and the method of achieving that goal.

The first part of her message has the phrase: 'If you want peace of mind'. Why did she judiciously use the word 'peace'? Instead, she could have used words like money, power or possessions—things that are generally desired. But then, is she not conveying that peace is the goal of human life? Here we also note that Mother's saying, '... If you want peace...' does not refer to peace that is temporary and transient, but uninterrupted bliss or unadulterated peace. It is this kind of peace that will bring true satisfaction and fulfilment in our lives.

If uninterrupted bliss is the ultimate goal of all human endeavour, then how do we, worldly people, engaged as we are in our worldly pursuits, proceed towards achieving such a state?

The second part of Mother's teaching tells us, '...do not find fault with others.' She is exhorting us to curb the tendency to criticize and deplore others. We blame God, the stars, the omens, and fate for all the troubles in our lives. We blame our parents for not bestowing the material comforts that we crave and lack. We blame our teachers for not 'educating' us enough. We blame our younger siblings for not obeying and the elder ones for not caring enough. We blame our friends, our colleagues, our spouses, the Government, the weather, anyone and anything that we feel causes us hardship and is a hurdle in enjoying a peaceful state. Possibly, there is a way out of this blame-game. We have to accept the fact that we get what we deserve and there is no point in blaming anyone or any situation.

Love is a potent factor in smoothening human relationships. Love allows growth and does not judge the individual based on one stray incident. An illustration comes in handy. Do we not see that a mother often overlooks the faults of her beloved child? No matter what her child may do, she never loses hope, always sees only the good aspects and apparently overlooks the faults altogether. This is a direct result of the immense love and concern that the mother has for her child. There is so much love towards the child that it burns away all possibilities of fault-finding. Love is the first step to get over the tendency of fault-finding.

The second step involves an expansion of our love so as to make us feel one with all around us—not just with those who are close to us through ties of family or friendship. The Holy Mother demonstrated this principle of spiritual and universal love throughout her life.

The above logic of expanding love is fine but the question still remains unanswered at this stage, as to how to practically develop supreme love towards all and yet be aware of our duties; especially when external disturbances and provocations add on to the inner turmoil ever raging within us. Ordinarily, we are so wrapped up in our own selves that we scarcely think of others, let alone feel great love for them! The Holy Mother again shows us the way out by telling us in the same message '...find your own faults.' Trying to look for faults within our own selves is the means to achieve an inner purification, which, as a natural consequence, will bring out the sort of universal love that we are trying to cultivate. And the most effective way to find our own faults is through the practise of constant introspection.

Introspection means regular watching of one's own thoughts. Once we cultivate this habit, we will have the adequate strength to detect our own faults. Even a little bit of introspection will reveal that there exists a basic tragedy in our lives—the inability to do that which we know to be right and helpful and the inability to avoid that which we know to be wrong and harmful. Duryodhana once said, '*Janami dharmam na cha me pravrittih, janami adharmam na cha me nivrittih*'—I know what is dharma but am unable to follow it and I know what is *adharma* but I cannot avoid it. The path of evil always appears easier and attractive. Unless we are sound in values, we shall not be able to hold on to truth, unselfishness, and so on. It is human nature to avoid the difficult. Being aware of this will help build our resolve to improve our lives through the practise of good and helpful actions. This is why the Holy Mother said; to have peace we must detect our faults. The energy that we waste in finding the faults of others will automatically get channelled to firm up our will-power and enable us to think clearly and live rightful lives. This gives us the much needed internal strength to face any kind of uninvited botheration inflicted upon us. Of course, introspection cannot be achieved in a single day—it has to be cultivated over several years. It requires immense patience and perseverance. Introspection and its process have been explained separately in this book.

The last part of the Holy Mother's message says, 'Learn to make the whole world your own. No one is a stranger, my dear; the whole world is your own.' How she exemplified this truth in her personal life is shown in the following incident. Once, during Durga Puja, she asked a disciple to purchase some cloth for her brothers' children. India was under the British rule then and Mahatma Gandhi's Satyagraha movement had urged Indians to boycott foreign goods, as a peaceful and non-violent protest against foreign rule. The disciple, influenced by this idea, bought cloth of Indian make only. But the women of the family disapproved of it and said that they wanted the better quality, foreign cloth. The disciple, out of patriotic feeling, replied in an excited voice, 'But what you want are all foreign clothes! How can I buy them?' The Mother was present there. She said, 'My child, they (the Westerners) too are my children. I must accommodate everyone. Can I ever be exclusive? Bring the clothes that they want.' Here, Mother reveals the highest truth of Advaita Vedanta, shining in all its glory and reminds us that ultimately all are one. Differentiations such as mine, yours, another are simply projections of the mind. Universal love becomes possible only when we can erase all dividing lines.

In this age of constant strife and turmoil, where no two communities can see eye to eye on any topic of mutual interest, leave alone live together in peace, this aspect of the Mother's last message has great significance for us. According to Mother, we are all part of one big family. After all, did she not say that she is the Mother of all? This makes all of us literally brothers and sisters! It is only this realization that can bring about peace in this world torn by wars and violence. Each one of us needs to understand the true significance of this message and must also spread it around.

One cannot help feeling great awe at the ramifications of Mother's last message. It not only contains instructions to achieve individual peace, but also prescribes the cure for all worldly problems and shows us how to achieve world peace! It is indeed a universal message—not just in its breadth, but also in its depth.

We know how throughout history, the avatars and messengers have spread their message wonderfully among the common masses, as per the needs of the time. However, the onus is on us to accept the message and then work hard to implement it in our lives. We have the Holy Mother's assurance that she will guide and protect us along the way. She once told a devotee, 'I am the mother of the wicked, as I am the mother of the virtuous. Whenever you are in distress, just say to yourself "I have a mother."' On another occasion, she re-emphasized this by saying that 'I shan't be able to turn away anybody if someone addresses me as Mother.' What a gloriously simple message Mother has left for us! All that we need to do is turn to her with complete surrender and whole-hearted love and she herself will give us enough strength and resources to realize our goal. Not just strength, Mother has assured us that she herself will do all that is necessary to make us realize our goals. All that we need to do is to accept her as our true Mother!

Just as a small child is completely dependent on its mother for all its wants, we too must turn to our eternal Mother. And like a small child sitting on its mother's lap, we must rely on her completely for guidance and protection. Past failures and sins need not make us feel despondent for we are in her care and a child does make mistakes knowingly or unknowingly. The Mother knows her child and will love it nonetheless. In this current incarnation, the Mother has gone past even the usual religious criteria of demanding absolute purity by saying, 'If my child wallows in dust or mud, it is I who have to wipe all the dirt off its body and take it in my lap.' No other avatar has ever given such an assurance! Even Sri Ramakrishna, who was the embodiment of divine grace, tested his disciples so much before accepting them. But in the Mother's case, all that is needed is that we must accept her as Mother.

Mother: This single word encompasses a tremendous emotional volume of love, selflessness, sacrifice, security, and calm repose.

Part I

The Essence of Life Management

3
Know the Ultimate Goal of Your Life

'What is the goal of it all? Can senses ever be the goal? Can enjoyment of pleasure ever be the goal? Can this life ever be the goal of the soul? If it is, better die this moment; do not want this life! If that is the fate of man, that he is going to be only the perfected machine, it would just mean that we go back to being trees and stones and things like that. Did you ever hear a cow tell a lie or see a tree steal? They are perfect machines. They do not make mistakes.'

—Swami Vivekananda

When we speak of the goal of life, most of us think of some worldly ambition. We say, 'I want to be an engineer', 'I want to be rich', and so on and so forth. We are so preoccupied in achieving our respective ambitions that we hardly explore what we really want in life. After working day and night, and struggling very hard, a person may become an engineer or a doctor, may amass wealth, and have a good family too. But do these guarantee happiness and peace that is eternal? Is this all that is there to life? What is the purpose of our existence? Most of us remain unaware about the ultimate goal of human life.

Within each of us is a natural urge to struggle for a better state of life than the present one. With regular practise of introspection we sense incompleteness in the current state of life. This makes us crave unalloyed happiness, uninterrupted peace, and immortality. This is the inner quest and ultimate goal of every human heart. We are all trying hard to attain it in our own way, irrespective of whether we are aware of our efforts in this direction and whether or not we succeed in our efforts during our lifetime.

We therefore work towards gaining a sense of completeness that we find missing in our lives. Generally we want to achieve something which we think is within our reach, except for some courageous men and women who like to make a sort of pole-vault to attain what is apparently beyond an individual's capacity. They are able to reject the alluring and prolific material goals, and focus only on the ultimate goal. Such people are very rare. Most of us are unmindful of the ultimate goal of life and set out to seek the desired completeness in life by pursuing material and tangible goals such as academic qualifications, a respectable career, marriage, progeny, creation of wealth, and so on—though not necessarily in the given order. This we do ignorantly or intentionally, following social conventions or a kind of herd mentality, with the underlying belief that by working hard and achieving some position of importance in social life, we will be able to achieve a state that is different from the present one; a happier, freer, more peaceful, more powerful and less miserable state.

But can we say that after working hard for so many years, earning much money and the respect of all those who surround us, we are really happy and satisfied? If it were so, then the so-called achievers and the successful—artists, administrators, managers, entrepreneurs, politicians, and many others would be the happiest people around. This is not necessarily true. A monk carrying out social welfare activities for the underprivileged had to coordinate with the concerned government office. At the office, he happened to ask a clerk if he was satisfied with his position in life. Not surprisingly, the man expressed utter dissatisfaction and wished for more money and power. Out of curiosity, the monk asked the clerk's superior, the Under Secretary, the same question. Funnily enough, here too the answer was exactly the same. In fact, when the monk met another senior officer, the Secretary, he still got the same answer! How is it that the satisfaction level of the senior officer is no better than that of a common clerk? What then has been achieved by studying so hard and clearing the competitive exams for entry into the hallowed portals of the prestigious Indian Administrative Services or working hard for so many years to achieve the much sought-after position of a Secretary to the Government?

Material Goals are not the Ultimate Goals of Life

The above anecdote tells us that joy and satisfaction, resulting from a pursuit of material success in order to gain a secure life, are short-lived. Sooner or later, we are impelled, almost involuntarily, towards pursuing some other material desire.

Chasing satisfaction and happiness through our many pursuits is like chasing a mirage in a desert. Illusions attract us and the ultimate goal eludes us throughout our earthly existence. We behave like the poor goat that has a stick tied to its head with some green grass dangling on the other side of the stick, before its eyes. No sooner does the goat move forward to eat it, the delicious and enticing grass also moves away by the same distance! The attraction of the grass compels the goat to keep up the chase until it finally drops down in sheer exhaustion. The poor goat is unable to realize that chasing the grass is a futile exercise and no matter how much it chases, the end result is frustration and disappointment. In this regard, a rich businessman or a Nobel laureate scientist may be as unfulfilled as an ordinary beggar on the street!

One of the reasons why happiness eludes us is because, at different times in our lives, we develop strong attachments to many material goals and their respective pursuits. When we achieve any one of our big dreams, we mistakenly assume that we have found the ultimate goal of our life. But we soon realize this joy is impermanent and set out to pursue yet another goal with the same idea of finding satisfaction. Of course, each time we find, not satisfaction but the same old sense of dissatisfaction and ennui.

While in junior school, we look up to our seniors and wish to be free and joyous like them. When we reach senior school, we find that life in senior school does not quite match our expectations and so we then dream of the wonders of college life. Again, college life turns out to be dissatisfactory and we then dream of making it big in our careers and enjoying heaps of money and power. When this too fails, we turn to wives or husbands and children for succour. Thus it goes, on and on; like an itch that cannot be cured through any amount of scratching. Our hunger for satisfaction torments us till the funeral pyre.

The more we chase material goals the more we suffer. We tend to compare ourselves with those who are better off than us in material comforts. This is the usual cause of our miseries. A person may get a certain job with a good salary, but the moment he sees his neighbour getting even more money, he becomes depressed and gloomy and starts feeling miserable.

Indeed, if achieving such material goals were the true purpose of human existence, we would not feel impelled to pursue other goals having once achieved them. If a person's goal is to become a doctor, then he should be fully satisfied on attaining this goal and should not need to work further. Yet, once he becomes a doctor, his goal changes to that of earning name, fame and wealth. This means that the goal of becoming a doctor was not the ultimate goal and there is some other deeper goal, which is driving him. The very definition of the word goal means the end of the race; there is no need to run further. A bit of introspection will reveal that behind all our impulses, all our hunger and lust for material objects lies the one, true desire for completeness—in other words satisfaction, fulfilment or peace.

According to Swami Vivekananda, uninterrupted peace is our true nature and we are all struggling to return to it. People call it by different names such as God or Brahman or Allah; but whatever the name, it is only this peace that we seek. The moment we find it, all our struggles, all our desires and joys and sorrows come to an end.

The Importance of Material Goals in Life

However, we should also guard ourselves from the feeling that these material goals are useless and therefore not worth struggling for. It is perfectly normal to desire a good career or a good education or even wealth, so long as it is earned through proper means. The many intermediate goals in life are necessary to at least obtain food and security and to provide for the needs of the human body. Hindu scriptures give due recognition to them. They prescribe four necessities—*Dharma* or righteousness, *Artha* or wealth, *Kama* meaning desire and *Moksha* meaning the state of uninterrupted peace, which is the ultimate goal. Thus we are allowed to pursue wealth and materialistic desires through righteous means.

The problem starts when we believe that it is only wealth and material desires that constitute the be-all and end-all of life. Our worldly attachments strengthen each time we achieve intermediate goals. In the process we forget all about moving towards the final human goal. Because of this attachment, we are not able to enjoy the material goals too. A small child is extremely happy when offered a toffee. If we try to snatch it away, the baby cries as if the whole world is coming to an end! To the child, the toffee is the most important thing in the world. This holds good for a child whose mind is yet to develop. However, it is a real tragedy to see grown-ups behave in this fashion. A grown up, dancing with joy on getting admission into a dream college, is not very different from the child we just mentioned! Undoubtedly, it will enable him to get a good job and hold his head high in society. But if he gets carried away and forgets about his ultimate goal, you can be certain that one day, when some other desire of his is not fulfilled, he will be broken-hearted and dejected.

Introspecting regularly helps us understand that our various earthly desires are only intermediate goals and that none of them is the ultimate goal. Religion provides us tools such as prayer, meditation, introspection, and so on. We should use them faithfully, for they provide us the ABCs of a life guided by ethics and enlightened living. Faith alone can remove our weakness and inspire us to do heroic acts. Swami Vivekananda said, 'The world is a grand moral gymnasium wherein we have all to take exercise so as to become stronger and stronger spiritually.'

We Should Seek 'Uninterrupted Peace' Even While Chasing Intermediate Goals

It is not wrong to resort to various intermediate goals in order to support our dependants. The Hindu scriptures have provided for *artha* and *kama* to be acquired by *dharmic* means. On the way, however, we need to strengthen ourselves so that we can attain our ultimate goal *moksha* too. This strength gives us the courage to face life's many challenges, without which one will be completely at the mercy of the external environment and will never be able to develop a strong personality.

The world will have selfish people who do not think twice to use foul means to achieve their ends, given even half a chance. But every society will have at least a few who are conscious of the means that can be used to reach the end. Such a life pattern is possible only for those who are morally strong and determined. Man, weak by nature, sometimes succumbs to temptations and abandons the right path in spite of knowing what is wrong. Being forced to go astray by his previous tendencies and ruling desires, he is haunted by nagging guilt.

Businessmen and professionals appear to adopt foul means in order to achieve worldly success, prosperity, and status. Some argue that such dishonest persons are respected in society and poor souls who try to follow honest means, seem to end up losing out in life. But look within their mind and you will see the former group tense, with dark clouds hovering in their mind. They are not masters but slaves to their passions. The latter have the wealth of values rather than money and are more powerful than our 'successful' friends, in limiting their desires. Medical research has shown that modern day ailments such as depression and feeling of worthlessness arise from life patterns that are motivated by short-term goals of money and pleasure. Such people fail to realize that by cheating their conscience and suffering from guilt they cannot lead peaceful lives! Honest people hesitate to do anything considered 'wrong'. They are aware that sooner or later they have to face their own mind and cannot run away.

In fact, it is true that somewhere in the depths of our consciousness we realize that material goals are intermediate, not final, and pursuing such temporary goals through dishonest means brings not peace but sorrow. The unconvinced person would argue that the fruits of evil or good deeds do not accrue in this very life, for evil people seem to live luxurious and comfortable lives while good people have to struggle all along. This tacitly points to the theory of reincarnation, which states that we have to face the consequences of all our actions either in this life or in future lives. Hesitation to commit foul deeds means that we subconsciously accept the fact that actions bring forth results, good or bad.

We Must Constantly Remind Ourselves to Seek Only 'Uninterrupted Peace'

We need to inculcate the habit of constantly reminding ourselves of the ultimate goal, through introspection and practise of SDM, which are emphasized throughout the book. Failures can haunt us and we may be troubled by jealousy and inferiority complex that comes from comparing ourselves to others who have achieved material success in life.

What happens when one forgets the ultimate goal? Let us think of a person who has not received his much desired promotion. When the promotions are announced, he finds that he has been overlooked and someone else has got the job. Now, if the man thinks that this material goal of his is the most important thing in life, he will naturally be very disappointed and may feel frustrated and depressed. His personality as a whole may undergo a change, there may be trouble in his married life, and he may lose his friends. However, if he remembers that this promotion is only an intermediate goal, he will not be so adversely affected, and will adapt himself to the situation. He may use the opportunity to find himself a better job, rather than succumbing to depression. Of course, it is very difficult to remain poised when we fail to achieve a cherished goal, but being aware of the real purpose in life can reduce our suffering.

In Conclusion

To summarize, a feeling of incompleteness within each one of us impels us to seek material goals. All such goals are only intermediate, and achieving them are akin to achieving milestones on our way to the ultimate goal of uninterrupted peace. For example, reaching the ultimate goal in life is like travelling from some far-off location to let's say, Delhi. Some of us may make the journey by air, whereas others may choose to travel by train or on road. Depending on the route and the mode of transport, there may be stops at various cities along the way. However, each traveller only passes through these intermediate destinations and is ever conscious of his true destination. Likewise, various intermediate goals in our lives should be likened to the many stations and stopovers on our journey towards uninterrupted peace, which is the ultimate and only true goal of life. All sincere efforts will be rewarded. No force can deny the reward that true effort brings about. With perseverance and dedication we shall reach the goal today or tomorrow. Patience pays.

Remembering that our ultimate goal is an inner pursuit of perfection within ourselves and not a material and transient one, helps in curbing jealousy and frustration, and enables us to function better. Arrogance and ego, often found in successful people, hinder progress. A few rupees do not enhance a person's ultimate value! Sri Ramakrishna once said that people have so many desires and so much ego, yet, after death, all that is left is one pound worth of ashes and a few bones! This will be the condition of all—the greatest king, the poorest peasant, our best friend and worst enemy. Remembering this, we should control our emotions and advance steadily towards the ultimate goal.

Our lives and our pursuit of material goals need to be designed with the ultimate goal in mind. Sri Ramakrishna remarked, 'The only purpose of life is God realization... if you put fifty zeros after one, you have a large sum. But erase the one and then nothing remains. It is the one that makes many.' God realization alone can give us uninterrupted peace while all the intermediate goals are like the zeroes. In the next chapter, the focus is on the practise of introspection as a tool to better ourselves.

4
Introspect to Improve

'Don't find fault with others. Rather learn to see your own faults.'

—Holy Mother Sri Sarada Devi

Introspection is very important and merits elaboration. When a schoolboy fares badly in his exams, his parents often tell him to introspect and find out the reasons for his poor performance. Similarly, when someone commits an evil act, the elders and seniors advise him to introspect, in order to help him realize the effect of his actions and so that he may avoid repeating similar mistakes in future. Evidently, introspection is a useful tool for one's betterment. It is because we lack the power of introspection that we often find ourselves feeling miserable.

Introspection and Its Importance

Introspection is the watching of one's own thoughts and emotions so as to be able to understand the source of all distractions and mental turmoil. It is the examining of

4

one's thoughts, to discriminate between good or beneficial thoughts and evil or harmful thoughts. Introspection is the art of thinking about one's own thoughts!

Diseases, aches and sprains make us suffer physically, whereas anger, jealousy, stress, depression and lack of concentration are some of our mental afflictions. For curing our physical ailments we visit a doctor who usually insists on a battery of blood tests, X-Ray scans, and CT scans, so much so that we are at times irritated and wonder if the doctor is ever going to treat us instead of sending our already tired bodies to different departments of the hospital! The truth is that the good doctor is only doing his job. He must first identify the problem before he can provide the cure. This process of finding the cause of the disease is known as diagnosis. In fact, once the diagnosis is successful, the disease is as good as cured in most cases. Similarly, most of our mental ailments are cured the moment we are able to find the cause, through accurate diagnosis. This diagnosis of mental ailments is known as introspection.

The crucial difference between our physical and mental ailments is that while we have medicines, hospitals, doctors and nurses to help us treat physical sickness, there is really nobody who can cure us of mental sickness. We can at best get some guidance from people like psychologists or psychiatrists but ultimately it is our own efforts that will help cure us. We have to become our own doctor and make full use of introspection, which is the most effective (and in fact, only) tool available to us. Introspection is also a form of prevention because when we practise it regularly, we become strong enough to ward off mental diseases even before they appear. This makes introspection even more important, since prevention is better than cure!

Introspection and Its Practice

Initially, we need to watch and be aware of the flow of thoughts in our mind. To start with, we must spare at least ten minutes, both in the mornings and evenings everyday. During those ten minutes, we should simply watch our thoughts without any reactions whatsoever. No censure, no criticism; simply accepting the way we are and making no efforts to change. Just watch the thoughts flow in and out of your mind, like a gateman, who watches people enter and leave the gate without speaking or reacting. Once we know the preoccupations, tendencies and inclinations of our mind through regular practise, we can guide it to our own advantage. This practise is further explained in the appendix.

Introspection also strengthens us to face life's great challenges. All of us have to face great tragedies at some time or the other. For some, the experience comes early in life while for others it may come later. Perhaps someone's parents have passed away at an early age or another is suddenly widowed after two decades of happy and blissful married life. When tragedy strikes, an individual may emerge stronger and purer than before, or may simply collapse. One may resort to alcoholism and drug abuse and thereby end up as a mere shell of a human being. This happens when we fail to examine the source of our sorrows and therefore get swept away by the tidal wave of grief that overcomes us. However, when we realize that we need to shake off this unhappiness and move on in life, we are able to use tragedy as an opportunity to strengthen ourselves and build our character. This is an instance of the practical benefit of the art of introspection.

If we regularly analyse the very world we live in, we can strengthen the habit of introspecting. Most of us take this world for granted and imagine that others must see and feel the same way as we do. This is grossly incorrect. In fact, each one of us lives in a different world. That is why the same object produces different emotions in different people. A father may feel deep love and affection when he sees a toy belonging to his own child, lying by the roadside, in front of his house. A stranger on the other hand, may see the same as a dirty doll, worthy of being kicked into the drain!

Again, we see how babies have no idea of the value of money and may even tear a five hundred rupees note into pieces without giving it a second thought. Yet things considered precious by a baby, such as a piece of toffee or an old, broken toy are useless for us. Even the same person, at different times, sees things in different ways. For instance, a child that claims his mother to be the best in the world when she lovingly serves food or puts him to bed or fulfils his desires, will see her as the world's worst mother when she gets angry at him, and scolds or slaps him. Or, consider a young couple professing undying love for each other and marrying against the will of their parents. But a few years later the same couple may publicly accuse each other like sworn enemies and end their marriage in a bitter divorce!

We have been led to believe that it is only the external environment that is responsible for all our evil tendencies and that it has much influence over us. But the above examples show that the mind projects its own thoughts and feelings onto the world around it. Our mind affects and distorts our perceptions of people and things. We perceive them different from what they actually are. It is through this coloured prism that we see objects and people around us and label them good or bad.

Our mind exerts such firm control over us that we get carried away and appear to have no say in the decisions that we take. Our mind leads us to believe that the world must run according to our plans, that we must be successful in all our endeavours and that people must be polite and sympathetic towards us. When reality dawns, we realize this is not always true. Adverse reactions often dishearten us and make us cynical. Introspection makes us realize that the world has no power to influence us unless we allow ourselves to be influenced.

Introspection and Control of Mind

The ability to find the source of suffering and seek possible solutions comes by introspecting. The source of all problems can be traced to the mind. A person went to the doctor and complained of pain. When the doctor asked him where the pain was, he touched various parts of his body with the right index finger and said that he had pain in all those places! The doctor examined and could not find anything wrong. The doctor then examined the index finger and found that the tip was fractured! So, the cause of pain was in the fingertip and not in the rest of the body!

The mind acts upon and further strengthens the inherent tendencies and inclinations during our interactions with the outer world. Generally, the mind acts as an agent of the lower self— the aspect of our personality that tries to drag us down and leads us to entertain evil emotions. It is a great enemy of the higher self—the aspect of our personality that inspires us to inculcate good habits and pure emotions.

Our mind often deceives us in many ways. Sometimes it cooperates; suddenly it springs a trap and destroys all our good intentions. Thus we need mind-control and the only way to control an undisciplined and harmful mind is to practise introspection regularly.

Analysis of everyday incidents will show how introspection helps control the mind. An average student who has not developed the capacity required to control his mind, will waste his time in activities such as gossiping and watching television, out of ignorance and carelessness. But the sudden awareness of approaching exams makes him realize that he will fail unless he studies hard. During that period, he allows nothing to distract him from his studies, not even his mother's call for food! He is able to achieve this level of control over his mind because exam-fear makes him realize the danger ahead, leading to introspection. When an individual becomes fully convinced of the utility of a particular path or action, he or she puts the best pos-sible effort to succeed. This is also seen in the case of the smoker who suddenly realizes one fine morning that his habit is harmful. If he is sincere, from that day he makes repeated efforts to quit the habit. Repeated actions form habits and the only way to get rid of bad habits is to engage oneself in actions that counter the bad habits. There are many examples of people who have been able to give up one or more bad habit and acquire good habits because they are convinced of the beneficial effects of their actions.

The Impulse-Thought-Action Sequence

Performing any action involves a three-step process, which we term an impulse-thought-action sequence. An impulse to perform an action arises first and is followed by a series of thoughts in our mind, which motivate us to perform that particular action. The propelling forces behind the impulse are our desires and previous experiences. The inclination or tendency to perform an action, coupled with our desires and memory of past experiences must get the consent of the will to actually culminate in an action. Seeing an ice-cream bar gives knowledge of the object. Then, desire to eat it crops up because somebody has told us that it tastes good. The will now gives direction to this thought by attaching the ego to it and we say, 'I want to eat that ice-cream.' The action to be performed must have our consent, which originates from a series of thoughts that follows the rise of the impulse in the mind. It is only after passing through these two stages that we can perform any action. At the initial stage when the tendency to act arises, the emotion emerges in the form of a bubble on the surface of our mind. At this stage it is easy to control and overpower that particular emotion. However, the bubble soon turns into waves, grips the mind and blinds us. These waves of emotion are then almost impossible to control.

For example, we may be annoyed at someone or something. This is the bubble-stage of anger. And then follows the stage when we become anger itself, with a red face, flaring nostrils, and so on. This is equivalent to the ripples-stage, which is a forceful flow of the anger emotion. Anger overpowers us only because we allow the impulse to grow. The trick is to stop consenting at the bubble stage itself and not entertain the thought further. This prevents the wave from taking shape. The catch is that this bubble-to-wave conversion takes a fraction of a second only and this is all the time we have to prevent an evil tendency from overpowering us and putting us in a position of great danger or embarrassment. Mastery of the mind requires split-second action and this can be developed from the practise of introspection.

We are aware that both good and bad tendencies exist within us. These tendencies are based on the impressions of our past actions and also on the stimuli emanating from our external environment. Our bad tendencies or bad influences must not dishearten us. Instead, we should stand firm and refuse to allow them to control us further.

A German philosopher has said that the tendency to sin is not a sin; it is the consent to sin that is a sin. We may feel the urge to commit bad actions; yet, this urge in itself is not a sin. It is only when we consent to the urge and go ahead to carry it out that the actual sin is committed. For instance, your parents want you to help your younger brother in his studies at a time when you wish to be out with your friends. Obviously, you are reluctant to comply and thus feel an impulse to lie or use some pretext to escape. Although the thought of telling a lie has appeared in the mind, the sin has not yet been committed. Firmly placing the principle of truth before you, fight off the evil tendency and make all efforts to be honest and pure in your approach. You must repeatedly refuse to give consent to evil tendencies, no matter how frequently or how forcefully they appear in your mind. Through this process you can strengthen your will-power and the power of discrimination.

Our inability to do what we know to be right and helpful, and avoid that which we know to be wrong and harmful must not be used to justify our misdeeds. Introspection helps build our resolve to improve our lives by the practise of good and helpful actions. We must stand up and face our weaknesses. We must take responsibility for changing our lives and should give up making feeble excuses such as, 'My friend influenced me to behave that way' or 'I don't know how it happened'. We must acknowledge that we ourselves are responsible for our actions. Our scriptures say that the effects of our actions will surely find us one day, even as a calf finds its mother amongst a herd of a thousand cows. 'As we sow, so shall we reap', that is, the fruits of actions will surely come to us sooner or later. If we perform righteous actions, we will be rewarded and will enjoy peaceful and fulfilled lives. If we perform unrighteous and evil deeds, we will suffer, feel miserable and wretched all our lives.

We must be awake at all times through the practise of introspection. Beginners may find it useful to maintain a daily diary with two columns—one for time wasted and one for time utilised in rightful activities. Analyse your entries at the end of each day and it will give you an insight on how time gets wasted, and this awareness will also enable you to flow your energies in the right direction.

Introspection: The Bottom Line

The problem is that we lack conviction and faith in the prescribed methods to improve our lives. That introspection can effect a change in our lives is now undisputed.

The mantra or the bottom line is—'Introspect daily, detect diligently, negate ruthlessly, substitute wisely, grow steadily and be happy.' What this means is that through continuous introspection we must detect the source of our suffering; once it is detected we must negate it ruthlessly and substitute it wisely with good thoughts and ideas. By doing so, we will grow steadily and will eventually attain to happiness. This is what Swami Vivekananda meant when he said that we must 'Arise, awake and stop not till the goal is reached.'

5
Manage Your Thoughts

'We are what our thoughts have made us; so take care of what you think. Our thoughts make things beautiful, our thoughts make things ugly.'

—Swami Vivekananda

Introspection, as described in the previous chapter, gives us the ability to determine the inner workings of that most wonderful faculty—the mind. Once a person is well established in the art of introspection, he will be able to see the type of thoughts that pass through his mind and assess if he has been able to cultivate a healthy mind.

Since most individuals never seriously attempt developing their mind, practise of introspection will bring out many thoughts that are not really to our liking. We may find unhealthy passions such as anger or jealousy eating into our mental energies. This discovery then transforms into the desire to somehow rid ourselves of these mental diseases and to renew ourselves so that we can be true masters of our own mind.

Understanding the Importance of Managing Thoughts

In order to use any machine efficiently and properly, we need to study its operating manual first. Similarly, if we wish to properly use this mind-tool for our betterment, we need to study and understand it fully.

We have seen that action is always preceded by a thought or feeling that motivates it. For instance, before I can eat food, the feeling of hunger and thought of food must arise in my mind. If my mind is preoccupied with some work then, I will not notice even delicacies, as the thought that motivates my mind towards the food is absent. So, control of actions presupposes control of thoughts.

Our scriptures go even further and say that our mind is nothing but a flow of thoughts, just as a river is nothing but a mass of flowing water. If the water is polluted, the river is deemed impure; if the water is clean, the river is deemed pure. So, to purify the mind river, we must purify the thoughts flowing in it. This further brings home the importance of thought management towards building a healthy, integrated life.

It is 100% true that one's personality is shaped by one's thoughts. If our thoughts are good, we feel happy and radiate confidence and charm around us. If our thoughts are wicked, we will be constantly afraid of being discovered and therefore feel miserable. Evil thoughts make us radiate a repulsive aura. When we are in a good mood, no matter how dirty or crowded the environment around us, we are most likely to be peaceful and calm. On the other hand, when we are in a bad mood, even a beautiful hill station or lake fails to calm our disturbed mind.

It is important to realize the vital role that thoughts play in our lives since, only then will we start to control our thoughts.

Spiritual aspirants often complain that in spite of reading so many scriptures and practising so many different techniques such as *Pranayama*, and so on, they have not benefited much and remain the same as before. The principal reason is that such people don't pay any attention to the management of their thoughts. Swami Vivekananda has described their condition in a rather humorous quote, 'Before we can crawl half a mile, we want to cross the ocean like Hanuman! It cannot be. Everyone going to be a Yogi, everyone going to meditate! It cannot be. The whole day mixing with the world with *Karmakanda*, and in the evening sitting down and blowing through your nose! Is it so easy? Should *rishis* come flying through the air, because you have blown three times through the nose? Is it a joke? It is all nonsense.'

The main reason for suffering caused by unruly and undisciplined thoughts is that we allow negative impressions to enter into our mind through our eyes and ears. This is similar to the cities that dump their pollution unchecked, into the rivers, and then spend huge amounts to get rid of the toxic wastes!

Everyday we go to the school or college or office and indulge in gossip, consciously discuss sinful things with our friends, and after returning home, expect our mind to be pure and disciplined—this is impossible. Have you seen what happens when the master gives his dog full freedom to do whatever it likes? It soon becomes wild, and bites and chases everyone, and perhaps one day will bite its own master! The position of our mind is exactly like that. For any true student of Life Management, the eyes and ears must function solely as conduits of positive and ennobling impressions on the mind. Why waste time seeing a serial on TV when that same time can be spent reading a few paragraphs from a spiritual book? The serial will only fill the mind with dirty and wretched thoughts that will induce you to commit all kinds of foul deeds. Unfortunately, most people choose to spend 30 minutes or more, casually enjoying the cheap thrills of some serial and suffer the rest of the day because of the bad thoughts it induces. What could be more foolish than this?

Understanding the True Nature of Thoughts

Having understood the importance of thought management, let us delve into the subject a little more deeply.

A thought has two components—one is *aham vritti* (subject) and the other is *idam vritti* (object). *Aham vritti* is that part of the thought that relates to us and *idam vritti* is that part of the thought that relates to whatever is perceived as non-self, or, everything except self. For instance, in the sentence, 'I see a red ball', the *aham vritti* is the perceiver of the ball, myself. *Idam vritti* (non-self) is what is outside of me, or the red ball. So every thought is a mixture of *aham vritti* and *idam vritti*. There will be constant struggle in our mind if we continue to perceive non-self and cling onto it saying, 'this is mine, and it belongs to me'.

Thoughts can also be analysed from three different aspects—quantity, quality and direction.

By quantity of thoughts is meant the frequency of thoughts, or in other words, the number of thought-eruptions per second. In most people, this is very high and is a prime source of misery.

Quality of thoughts means the nature of thoughts that arise in our mind, such as good or bad thoughts, pure or dirty thoughts, selfish or selfless thoughts and so on.

Finally, by direction of thoughts, we mean the path of flow of thoughts. Thoughts tend to flow in one direction—if we are angry, then everything around us will appear faulty; if we are happy, then everything around us will seem joyous.

Controlling the Quantity of Thoughts

One of the basic facts of thought management is that the more the thoughts rushing into our mind, the more disturbed and unhappy we are. For instance, when we are angry or excited there is a sudden increase in the number of thoughts and as a result, we lose all control and commit acts that cause embarrassment or harm. When the quantity of thoughts is high, we are mentally disturbed and suffer from lack of sleep, bad digestion, headache, high blood pressure, tension, and so on. In fact, depression, dejection or remorse is due to higher number of thoughts. In extreme cases, high frequency of thoughts can also cause insanity.

Conversely, if thoughts are less in number, we experience peace and become calm and quiet. This is why we feel peaceful when we practise watching the flow of thoughts in our mind. This can also be evidenced by the fact that we enjoy great peace in deep sleep. In this state, thoughts cease to flow and the mind disappears, as it were, for a time. This results in great peace and when we awaken, refreshed and rejuvenated, we say, 'I don't know anything of what happened last night; I just know that I slept well.'

It should also be remembered that the greatest results are achieved only when we work with a calm and quiet mind. So in order to enjoy success in our endeavours, it is essential to cultivate a calm and quiet mind by reducing the number of thoughts.

A high quantity of thoughts, especially if they are unwanted ones, is an unnatural state and so it causes unhappiness. A mother gets tired of carrying around the vegetables and groceries that she purchases from the market. She may be carrying her three-year-old child also. Yet she never gets tired of her child, which weighs so much more! When she reaches her house and deposits the load and the child, stress vanishes and she feels light and free. Similarly, when the cultivated good thoughts are increased, quantity of thoughts in the mind increases but it does not cause strain. However, the load of unwanted thoughts when removed, will make one feel true peace and happiness.

Now in order to control the quantity of thoughts, two things are absolutely essential—discipline and meaningful engagement at all times.

Discipline, as we discuss it here, means the carrying out of one's activities in a planned and systematic manner according to a regular timetable. When we are disciplined, we don't waste time because, we don't need to plan and re-plan our activities. The mind gets calmed automatically when we discipline it and do not give in to its whims and fancies.

Although disciplining oneself all through the day is difficult, we must make a commitment to practise it for at least four to five hours a day. We should make a start in this way, till it becomes a habit. This sort of discipline will give a proper framework to our lives and will not allow our mind to react and get involved in unplanned activities.

The other important thing is to keep busy at all times—of course, busy in constructive, righteous and healthy activities! See how few thoughts run through your mind when you are busy writing an exam! The mind is so focused on finding answers to the questions that no unwanted thought enters the mind.

Fifty or sixty years ago, people in general were relatively happier than the present times! They would spend all their free time in household work. Some would even refuse to engage servants, saying that they wanted to serve their families out of love. Being busy, they had no time for gossip or the cinema and were relatively peaceful. Nowadays, people simply run after leisure and free time and then waste all that time in filling up their heads with stupid and unhealthy thoughts.

Being busy also means being alert. How alert we are when we drive a car! Other distracting thoughts are not allowed into the mind; the one and only thought that dominates is how to drive and reach the destination safely. If we remain similarly alert in all our activities, we will be able to keep out unnecessary thoughts from our mind to a large extent.

The same idea has been expressed in our scriptures in a slightly different fashion: 'Perform all your duties righteously'. Once we resolve to perform all our duties in various roles of son, father, mother, student, and so on properly, our mind will be so occupied that there will be simply no time for day dreaming!

Controlling the Quality of Thoughts

Thoughts can be either good or bad depending on their nature. Good thoughts inspire us to lead a noble life, a life guided by universal values. Bad thoughts propel us towards unhealthy and selfish activities.

If we spend the whole day associating with good people and things, our thoughts will naturally be good, and if we spend it with bad people and things, our thoughts will be bad. What is good and what is bad is determined by our own value systems and cannot be determined on the basis of social customs or popular perceptions. For instance, some people consider meat as a very healthy and nutritious food while others consider meat eating, a sin. Neither is right or wrong. It is just that the value systems are different and that causes a difference in outlook. However, when viewed from the standpoint of the ultimate goal as discussed in the first chapter, good associations take us closer to the ultimate goal, while bad associations take us further away. Ultimately, it is our discretion and discrimination that can help us from unwanted influences. We must decide to help ourselves.

The only way to improve the quality of our thoughts is to calm the mind. Our scriptures say that desire, anger, greed, delusion, jealousy and vanity are the six enemies of man and these must be conquered. When these inimical forces lose their power or are absent in us, our mind becomes peaceful. By calming the mind, the quality of thoughts can be maintained and this helps us gradually purify our thoughts.

Controlling the Direction of Thoughts

Our thoughts tend to flow in one direction and we often find it hard to change this. We are like a small child learning to ride a cycle. As long as the cycle moves in one direction, the child is fine; but when it tries to change the direction, it promptly falls down! The problem with us is that we have let our mind wander so habitually that it refuses to cooperate any longer.

The only remedy is to repeatedly expose ourselves to noble thoughts and ideas. Such exposure is more effective in strengthening our inner being than a vitamin pill. Saint Eknath changed the ways of his wayward son by introducing him to holy ideas.

Carelessness in choosing companions leads to suffering. In fact, our scriptures say that in this matter there must be no compromise—if we find a friend disturbing the mind, we must cut off all contact with him, no matter at what cost. The powerful influence of bad company is capable of snatching away all our good qualities. The company of those with bad tendencies will make us just like those people. Sri Ramakrishna Paramahamsa would often say that if garlic is kept in a vessel, the vessel catches its smell and it cannot be removed easily. It is said that it is better to live in the forest with the hill tribes than to live with a fool in heaven!

Satsanga or good company also has tremendous power and can build an unseen fort or wall around us to ward off unwanted thoughts. However, the problem is that we practise only weekend *Satsanga*, which in reality is weakened *Satsanga*! This is our condition and that is why there is no improvement. We like everything cheap—we pay five thousand rupees to attend some seminar on spirituality and believe that everything will be perfect henceforth. Without practise, there can be no improvement. Money cannot buy us peace.

Shankaracharya, in his famous work *Bhaja Govindam* says in a *shloka*, 'Satsangatve nissangatvam, nissangatve nirmohatvam, nirmohatve nischalatattvam, nischalatattve jeevanmuktih'—through *Satsanga*, one attains non-attachment, non-attachment leads to freedom from delusion, freedom from delusion leads to clarity of perception (i.e. freedom from desires) and perception of truth leads one to the liberated state. Such is the power of *Satsanga*.

Satsanga does not mean that one has to escape from the world and join some *ashrama*. Apart from being in holy company, it is to be cultivated in our mind by the study of good books, listening to spiritual talks and music, thinking of elevating thoughts, and so on. One may visit temples and *ashramas* on weekends when free, and during the rest of the week, *Satsanga* is to be practised by reliving the holy associations and activities. This is termed *manana* and *nidhidhyasana* in our scriptures.

Understanding the Three Motions of the Mind

After analysing the quantity, quality and direction of thoughts, it is necessary to know a subtler aspect: the movement of the mind in time, space and among objects. Just as we can control the quantity, quality and direction of thoughts, it is also possible to control these three movements of the mind.

Movement in time happens when we flit between thoughts of the past, present and future. While working in the office, memory of some incident from our childhood, an event that probably happened twenty years ago, may suddenly occupy the mind.

Movement in space happens when we flit from thoughts of one place to that of another. One may be sitting in the office but the mind may be thinking of a scene from the cinema.

Movement between objects happens when we flit from thoughts of one object to that of another. This minute we may be thinking of *rasagollas* and the very next moment our mind pictures a car!

When the mind is controlled from running in space, it is called *dharana*. To practise *dharana* effectively, one must concentrate the mind in one place, usually the region of the heart. This is not the same as the physical heart; there is also a spiritual heart located in the same region. Gradually, one acquires the power to dictate to the mind so that it stays in the heart and does not roam here and there while meditating. This will take a long time, but the practise can start immediately.

When the mind is controlled from running after objects, it is called *dhyana*. True meditation happens when the mind is concentrated on one object and held there. The object of concentration has to be chosen carefully. Our scriptures say that we become whatever we think of. If the object of concentration is not noble, the mind will be ultimately ruined by constantly thinking about it. The solution is to concentrate the mind on a holy person or object—to inspire and elevate it by refining our natural emotions into devotion and pure love. Those who receive initiation are given one particular *Ishta*, or Chosen Deity and they concentrate their mind on that *Ishta*.

Like in the case of *dharana*, *dhyana* too will take a long time to perfect—the important thing is to keep up the practise and to have patience.

Finally, when the mind is controlled from running in time, it is called *samadhi*. When we are deeply engrossed in some activity like studying for an exam or watching some favourite serial on TV, we lose count as time passes by. Such ordinary concentration in our daily activities is a succession of related thoughts on one subject with each thought not lasting more than a few minutes. In *dhyana*, there will be just one thought wave which when sufficiently prolonged, leads to *samadhi*. When the mind is held from running in time for a longer period, *samadhi* happens. The *samadhi* state cannot be explained, it has to be experienced.

Managing Thoughts by Practising Detachment

While closing this discussion, it is important to note that we can truly manage our thoughts only by practising detachment. If we are too attached to possessions and people, in spite of all our efforts, thoughts will always evade management and we will remain disturbed. Suppose there is a lose thread hanging from the shirt and we try to pull it out. What happens? If the thread is still attached to the cloth at the other end, pulling it will cause creases and spoil the shirt. The right approach is to cut at the other end of the thread so that it is also free and then the thread will slide out easily. Similarly, if we try to pull away the mind from all thoughts, without first detaching ourselves from the cause of these thoughts, we will not only face failure but also become prey to all sorts of mental ailments. It is important to note here that when some particular thought is bothering, there must be something or somebody behind that thought—there cannot be a thought without an object or subject behind it.

Let us say, you want to get over the feelings of lust or greed. At the same time, if you continue to watch TV, which relays programmes and advertisements that incite passions, then no matter how hard you try, you will never succeed in removing those feelings. One must first cut off the root or cause with the help of discrimination, if the tree of attachment is to be destroyed.

Many people do not understand this and attempt to practise meditation. When they sit down with closed eyes, they find that the number of thoughts has suddenly increased! Why? Because, their mind are so full of various thoughts and desires and when they close their eyes and try to concentrate, these thoughts are propelled forth with fresh vigour. It is not that meditation is ineffective; it is just that their practise cannot be effective and complete without acquiring detachment.

One has to first detach from all disturbing attachments and then attempt meditation. To strongly attach oneself to the *ishta* or some noble idea and thereby reduce the intensity of other useless bindings will make the process more enjoyable and peaceful! Detachment and its importance have been further discussed in Part II of the book.

Lack of self-awareness, resulting in lack of confidence and an abundance of fear in our mind is the prime source of unwanted and unnecessary thoughts that disturb our inner peace. A weak mind is always agitated and disturbed while a strong mind is tranquil at all times. All great spiritual masters are so peaceful because, they do not have weak personalities. They have realized their true nature and since their vision is clear, they have no fear or delusions. They are masters of their mind and emotions and this makes them peaceful always.

By sincerely following the tips set out here, the reader will gradually gain strength of mind and feel so strong and confident internally that all fear will vanish. He will then be filled with infinite peace and bliss.

6
Learn the Art of Action

'We are responsible for what we are; and whatever we wish ourselves to be, we have the power to make ourselves. If what we are now has been the result of our own past actions, it certainly follows that whatever we wish to be in future can be produced by our present actions; so we have to know how to act.'

—Swami Vivekananda

'Such is life, here today, gone tomorrow! Nothing goes with one, except one's merit and demerit; good and evil deeds follow one even after death.'

—Holy Mother Sri Sarada Devi

The *Bhagavad Gita* says, 'Verily none can remain, even for a moment without performing action.' Seen in this light, it is evident that activity is the sign of life. The sprouting of a seed or reaction of parents to a loving embrace of their child, are indications of the presence of life. A dead seed will not sprout, no matter how much water is poured on it. The moment action ceases, an organism is declared dead. Every single moment we are engaged in some work or the other, be it at school, college, office or home, irrespective of whether we are a sweeper, a housewife, a businessman, a student or a powerful executive by profession. Learning the 'Art of Action' will therefore help one and all.

What impels us to perform various actions all through our lives? The chapter, 'Know the Ultimate Goal of Your Life' has made it clear that a sense of incompleteness within each one of us is responsible for our varied desires. This in turn motivates us to work and perform actions in order to achieve different goals in life. For instance, a feeling that I am incomplete without a trendy car or the latest computer or a branded shirt would normally give rise to a desire in me to own these things. This would make me work to earn money and procure these items of desire. Similarly, others work to acquire degrees, a good job, and so on. Our own experience teaches us that such material gains can at best satisfy us only temporarily, for a few moments or a few days. Material achievements, termed intermediate goals, are necessary for our worldly existence and also for our journey towards the ultimate goal of life. Any work done or any action performed, even if it is towards achieving an intermediate goal, should bring us closer to a feeling of completeness and take us closer to our ultimate goal—the state of uninterrupted peace.

Art of Action: Distinguishing Work from Karma

The English word 'work' means the use of physical or body power to do something. We often say, 'I work at home' to mean domestic chores like cooking food, washing clothes, cleaning the house, and so on. We say, 'I work in office' when we have to conduct meetings, go on tour, and so on. Here, bodily effort is critical for carrying out whatever work we undertake. On the other hand, the Sanskrit term 'karma' means volitional action or action with intention. It is based on the recognition of man's power of judgement and his capacity to choose his course of action. As we shall see, 'action' here includes both mental and physical action and is therefore much broader than work. Thus, 'work' does not have the same significance as 'karma' and the two cannot be used interchangeably. There is a type of karma that is unintentional, such as sneezing, respiration, digestion, assimilation of food, and the like and these are not being discussed here.

To reiterate, any action motivated by some intention and accompanied by desire for its fruits is termed as 'karma'. In other words, karma is the work done by an individual with an intrinsic feeling that he or she is the doer of the work and that such work is done for the purpose of reaping the results of actions so performed.

We may further understand this subtle difference between work and karma through the following example. When a mother asks her child to fetch bread from the market, the child makes an excuse and says, 'I am not feeling well, I can't go.' Here the child is trying to escape from work by not performing the physical action, but has however not escaped from doing karma which was performed in the form of the mental manipulation through which he tried to trick his mother. Another example is that of a man who comes back tired from office and spends the entire evening simply sitting in front of the television. Apparently he is not doing any physical work, but still, his conscious decision to watch television is karma. Yet another example is when we are brooding on some problem. In such a case, no physical action is involved but the process of so many thoughts passing through our mind is karma.

Understanding the Law of Karma and the Concept of Rebirth

Having understood what constitutes karma, let us now turn our attention to the inviolable Law of Karma, which forms the bedrock of our existence and is therefore essential in our attempt to learn the Art of Action.

The Biblical phrase, 'As you sow, so you reap' is in essence the entire Law of Karma. Simply put, good karma brings good results and bad karma brings bad results. Righteous karma brings merit and leads to favourable conditions of life, while unwanted karma brings demerit and unfavourable conditions of life. None can escape the Law of Karma, whether he is a student or a doctor or a professor or a labourer.

Each one of us is reaping the fruits of our karma performed in the past. Our karma of today impacts our future, even determining the nature of that impact. Otherwise, why does a similar task evoke such diverse attitudes, approaches, efforts and results among individuals from similar backgrounds and social environments? This effect of karma in influencing the condition of one's life is also responsible for seemingly unfair situations in life. Swami Vivekananda said, 'What you have earned by your past actions, none can take away from you. If you have deserved wealth, you can bury yourself in the forest and it will come to you. If you have deserved good food and clothing, you may go to the North Pole and they will be brought to you. The polar bear will bring them. If you have not deserved them, you may conquer the world and will die of starvation.'

The Law of Karma requires us to believe in the concept of rebirth. According to it, only exceptionally good or exceptionally bad karmas have an impact in the present life, other karmas manifest in future lives. The residual effects of all accumulated karmas of one life are carried forward into our future lives. It is somewhat akin to the accounting practice where, the closing balance in the book of accounts of one accounting year is carried forward as the opening balance of the next year.

Using the Law of Karma to Solve the Riddles of Life

The Law of Karma can also be used to analyse human life and solve some of its greatest mysteries.

Every now and then we come across some uncommon talent or genius, which, try as we might, we cannot fathom. It is surprising to see a ten-year-old girl, playing a musical instrument, far better than the maestros of the day! Then there is the common example of two sons in a family—one of whom has grown up into a great and renowned doctor while the other has turned out to be a miserable failure, spending all his life by being dependent on others and creating trouble all around. A husband and wife leading an ideal life may have a blind child after a long wait, while another couple that lives by cheating and oppressing others is blessed with a sound and healthy child! We start to question the inconsistency, 'Why do good people suffer?'

Such painful realities make us question the very existence of God also. How can such injustice prevail if God is a just and merciful ruler? How can an omnipotent and omniscient God allow such paradoxes to exist? Isn't the very presence of evil a strong hint that God is only a figment of our imagination? Seeing such contradictions, there are many who give up faith and belief in the existence of God. Such an approach unfortunately makes us all the more miserable and keeps us ignorant of the real truth.

Our great sages and incarnations have said that regular introspection and detached observation will lead to the inevitable conclusion that there is no injustice and no undeserved merit or demerit in the world. All such incidents are actually the outcome of the past karmas. If we had the perception to see the past, we would understand the theory of rebirth, and perceive the perfect divine justice that exists in every corner of the infinite cosmos. The seers and spiritual masters, on the basis of their experiences, have concluded that birth, marriage and death are all predestined and the so called random events and chance encounters are part of the synchronistic behaviour of the universe. In reality there are no accidents! It is karma that determines our birth, our parents, brothers, sisters, conditions of life, and so on. This also tells us that if we wish to enjoy a peaceful life in the future, it is only our good karmas, performed in this life that can earn us that right.

To assert the truth of this argument, we present a situation involving two equally bright students who appear for an exam. Both performed equally well but one procured 98% and the first rank while the other secured 97% and the second rank. Their answer sheets were scrutinised by the same teacher! He checked the first paper in the morning, in a good mood and so gave 98%. Later in the day, he had an argument with his wife and so was in a foul mood when he checked the second student's paper. This student lost out on all the appreciation that went to the first student for topping the exam. Now who is to blame for this? It seems as if life has been unfair although both the students prepared equally hard and were equally competent. However, according to the Law of Karma, there is no unmerited gain or loss. We can only surmise that the first student had some righteous karma in his account and so life presented him with a favourable situation whereas the second student had some unrighteous karma in his account and therefore got an unfavourable situation.

Understanding the Impact of Actions on Character

An aspect of the law of karma is that every karma produces two results: one immediate and noticeable and the other remote and not noticeable in its present form. The results of mental karma are more powerful than that of physical karma. For instance, when a child burns its finger in fire, the immediate result is that it screams in pain. The remote result is the creation of a fear impression on its mind, making it wary of fire for the rest of its life. Another example is that of a girl who rescues a drowning child. While the immediate result is the appreciation she gets for her heroic deed, her hidden result is the set of impressions formed in her mind, which induce her to behave in a similar fashion in the future.

Thus whatever karma a person does—physical, mental or verbal, good or evil, produces two results. The second, remote result, in the form of an impression in the subconscious mind, dwells there as a potency and will inevitably fructify in due course. Obviously, the nature of impression created depends on the nature of the karma performed. Good karma leads to good impressions and bad karma to bad impressions. The collective impressions of our mind are called *samskaras* in Sanskrit and this fund of impressions, determines our personality. A person with predominantly good samskaras tends to have a good personality and the one with bad *samskaras* will have a bad personality.

Our *samskaras* influence our actions in various ways and all through our lives. Once, Sri Ramakrishna's father was called upon to bear false witness in a case and was threatened that if he did not do so, all his assets would be taken away and he would be sent out of the village. He steadfastly stuck to truth in spite of being aware of the consequences that he would have to face. He had such great moral strength and faith in God due to his positive samskaras.

How can we explain the colour preferences of babies when we find that some always choose red colour toys while others choose blue ones? Here we cannot say that the environment influences the choice because, the child's intellect is not yet developed to differentiate and discriminate, and then choose. Similarly, differences in personality, aptitude and character among siblings or identical twins cannot be explained on the basis of environment and upbringing. The only possible solution according to our scriptures is that these differences are due to the tendencies and latent impressions of karma, performed in previous births and acquired as *samskaras* in the current life. This also explains why we behave in a particular way in a given situation, as further demonstrated in the following incidents.

Suppose someone accidentally pushes another person on a street. A person with bad *samskaras* will immediately create a ruckus on the spot, whereas a person with good *samskaras* will either protest gracefully or simply ignore it. Or, consider a student who always succumbs to the temptation to cheat in an exam. Here too, he is a puppet in the hands of the evil *samskaras* or habit that force him to follow the wrong means. A thief, who lives his life in constant fear of being caught, will still make no effort to change his ways because of the tendencies or *samskaras* he has acquired in the past. Finally, think of a person who finds a purse lying in the temple premises. If he has good *samskaras*, he will immediately hand it over to the temple authorities and the thought of using the money for his own benefit will never cross his mind. However, if he has evil *samskaras*, he will not feel the slightest hesitation to pocket all the money.

Another aspect of this law is that the greater the interest of the doer in any activity, the deeper is the impression created. For example, all through the day we see many faces. Yet at the end of the day, it is probably only one of the faces that flash vividly before us! Possibly our interest in the person was triggered by something that we saw in this particular face—perhaps the similarity of a dear friend or of our mother.

A sad but true fact of our lives is that social conditioning, peer pressure or just plain curiosity makes us interested in activities like gossiping, watching meaningless television serials, and the like. On the other hand, our interest in activities that require discipline and concerted effort such as, regular physical exercise, reading of good literature, daily meditation, and so on, rapidly dwindles away. It is definitely possible to cultivate good habits and thereby free ourselves from the grip of bad samskaras. All that is required is perseverance and repeated efforts with the knowledge of our true self.

We need to make every possible effort to perform righteous karma and at the same time diminish our interest in evil things, thus reducing the possibility of unwelcome karma. It is entirely up to us to make the right choice and to strengthen our will through each small conquest.

Effective practice of the Art of Action requires us to sharpen our ability to remain constantly aware of the impressions in our mind and the karma we perform or are likely to perform. This awareness can only come from the practise of introspection. Such awareness will alert us the moment inimical impulses or desires arise in the mind, and we will gradually gain the ability to prevent ourselves from indulging in bad karma.

Unfortunately, we get carried away by our desires and impulses, and give in to hunger for immediate gratification of some desire, caring little for the long-term consequences, with the fond hope that we will somehow be able to escape them. Why else does a student avoid studies even when exams are near? He hides from his parents and reads comics instead of textbooks. Consequently, he fares badly in the exams and is unable to secure admission to a good college. He who started out by believing that he could cheat the law has instead cheated himself! His self delusion ruins his career. The Law of Karma pays little heed to the tricks by which we fool our parents or teachers or anyone else. Its only concern is with what we actually do—whether in public or in secret.

Understanding the Types of Karma

As mentioned before, the Art of Action is the control of actions to reverse the impulse-thought-action sequence. What kind of control we exercise over our actions can best be understood by first acquiring a comprehensive understanding of the nature of Karma. Hindu philosophy classifies Karma as *Agami* Karma, *Sanchita* Karma, and *Prarabdha* Karma. *Agami* Karma is the karma that will bear fruit in future lives. *Sanchita* Karma is the accumulated Karma of past lives. They do not bear fruit right now and one cannot say when they will fructify. *Prarabdha* Karma is that which is already bearing fruit in this life. They are the impressions of previous lives that have caused this life and fructify in this life.

The positive implication of this theory is that by controlling the karmas performed in this life, we can change the store of karmas or *Sanchita* karmas that determine our states in future lives. The classic example of an archer with a quiver of arrows is cited to illustrate human beings' control over their karmas. Just as the archer cannot control the arrow that has already been shot at the target from his bow, people have no control over their *Prarabdha* karmas. *Agami* karma is like an arrow that the archer has fixed to the bow and is about to shoot. If the archer chooses, he can remove the arrow and not shoot it at all. Finally, *Sanchita* karmás are like the arrows in the archer's quiver, which he can throw away if he so desires.

Of the three, *Prarabdha* Karma is the most important. It has the same effect on our lives as a sack of rocks carried on the back. No doubt, the load restricts movement and regulates the speed with which a person can move. However, freedom of movement is retained and at least the direction of movement can be decided, if not the speed of movement. So if our karma has been predominantly evil, the load is heavy and we move slowly. If the karma has been predominantly good, the load is light and we can move faster. In either case, the freedom to move in whatever direction we like is not impeded—this is our free will, our freedom of action.

Understanding Freedom of Action

Freedom of action is the ability to choose the course of action in a given situation. This special privilege, granted only to humans, distinguishes them from lower beings. Animals are guided only by blind instinct and are not capable of making a conscious choice, born of discrimination. A small boy when affectionately pulled by the ear is able to recognize it as a loving gesture and responds accordingly; but a dog when pulled by the ear, reacts angrily out of an instinct to protect itself. It is incapable of recognizing a gesture whose motive is only love and not enmity.

Unfortunately, humans rarely use this free will for constructive purposes. They misuse it, instead. Given a choice between going to the theatre for a worthless cinema and reading an inspiring book and visiting an *Ashrama*, most young people prefer dissipating themselves in a theatre! Similarly, when someone is unfair to us, instead of using the freedom of action to solve the problem in a calm and composed manner, we lose our cool, only to worsen the situation. It is only later that we repent. By then, the deed is done and the effect of our karma has already marked us out. Thus, we need to use this privilege of free will judiciously. We can use it to make or break our lives just as we can use fire either to cook food or to maliciously set aflame a house.

Man is accountable for all his deeds. However, he also has the freedom to act, not to act, or act in a different manner. His inner development depends on his choice to perform only those volitional actions that mould the personality through the formation of noble *samskaras*. Just as regular physical exercise is inevitable for physical development, so is the inner culture of making conscious decisions and remaining aware of our actions necessary for mental and spiritual development.

A question may be asked here. If every individual has freedom of action, does this not contradict God's sovereignty? The Law of Karma lays the whole responsibility of a man's actions on him only. Is there then no basis for the existence of God as a supreme ruler? If the Law of Karma can explain everything in life, where is the need to introduce a God? The answer is that individual freedom of action never interferes with God's supremacy. At the same time, it is also true that God's supremacy does not counter individual freedom. For example, no vegetation can grow without the sun—be it the sacred *tulsi* plant or the harmful poison ivy. All kinds of plants are allowed an equal opportunity to grow and blossom in the bountiful lap of Mother Earth under the same sun. Similarly, God enlivens all beings; individuals function according to their inherent potential only because of Him. None can work independently without Him, yet each man has the freedom to use God's power in his own way. It is like the power of electricity that can be used either for destructive or for constructive purposes.

Understanding Purushartha *(Self-effort) and* Prarabdha *Karma*

Let us explore the aspect of *Prarabdha* Karma's impact on our lives further. It is due to this that no two human bodies are exactly alike—even identical twins have some differences. We are born dark, fair, tall or short due to *Prarabdha* Karma. Although we have no freedom in choosing what type of body we have, who our parents will be, and so on, we must remember that we are basically the infinite spirit and that we have the potential to achieve all that we want. It is in human nature to struggle against all odds. Since nothing comes free in this world, it goes without saying that our karma is to make the best use of the opportunities that we have and cultivate a positive attitude to life and its problems.

We are not presenting a fatalistic view by saying that karma determines our life patterns. It is to lay emphasis on how we work, what work we do and how concerned we are about our own moral and spiritual development that the karma theory was explained. It is important to note that individual effort has the capacity to change things.

When a student fails his exams, his concerned parents arrange extra tuition for him and make him toil hard. As a result, the student gains confidence and is able to pass with decent marks in his next attempt. He succeeds because he decided to struggle in the right direction. When travelling to a high altitude destination, we take adequate woollens to protect ourselves from the chilling cold. It is unreasonable to take the stand that it is our karma to suffer because the decision to travel to a cold place was ours! Swami Vivekananda used to say that if we take care of the means, the end is assured. Nothing can stop it from accruing. This is logical too. One may be talented, but if the talents are not cultivated, sharpened and groomed through practice, even the finest of talent will go waste. Therefore, we need regular practice through self-effort, to effectively manifest our talents. This is a part of managing ourselves.

Effort or struggle to change one's life is known as *'purushartha'* or self-effort. The Art of Action requires us to develop an ability to discriminate between *purushartha* and *prarabdha* karma. The materialistic world judges one's position in society on the basis of his or her academic achievements, assets, possessions and wealth. Carried away by this, many young people are prone to weave all kind of fantasies about their futures without even realizing their inherent capabilities. They may develop deep dissatisfaction about the lack of facilities and opportunities in their lives. Such negative attitude does not help build life. It is essential that we have faith in our potential divinity and try to achieve the best in life. We must remember that material possessions do not make a man. How he sees himself, how he uses his body and mind, determines his life. Therefore it is said, 'God helps those who help themselves'. It is possible to change the effects of our *Prarabdha* through self-effort and sincere prayer to God, to help us in all our endeavours. It is good to dream of higher goals and aim to achieve them. If the target is high, our efforts will also be more. We shall then be able to achieve more than what we would by simply sitting and brooding about our karma.

An ideal balancing of *Purushartha* and acceptance of our *Prarabdha* rarely happens, resulting in a wide mismatch between what we dream of and what we actually achieve. Since most of us are unaware of our true abilities, we do not put in the required amount of effort required to achieve our goals. Most dream-ers therefore, continue to daydream. Growing old and finding their youthful energies frittered away, they are unable to withstand the pressure of life's hard reali-ties shattering their make-believe world. They fail to realize that success in any field comes only through hard work and God's grace. Without strong faith in one's own divinity or in God, it is impossible to avoid frustration when failure stares at us. We must learn to judge ourselves by the internal development that we have achieved and derive satisfaction and fulfilment from it. Life is a combination of both the external man and the internal man, and deficiency in any one area will weaken the person, especially if the true internal self is neglected.

The ability to use *purushartha* properly has special relevance for young men and women who are shap-ing their future careers. One should make all possible efforts diligently, sincerely and repeatedly to secure admission to a good college or to find a good job. Sup-pose that does not happen, then efforts must be made to get the next best college or job. The world is large and the opportunities are plenty. One failure does not mean the end of the world. Just as it may be our *prarabdha* to be denied one position, it must be our *prarabdha* to try and procure another! Karma is action and it does not accept a defeatist attitude. Everyone need not become a doctor or an engineer or a corporate executive. There is much more to life than these titles and other avenues can also provide us with decent lives. Ultimately, it is how we value ourselves that is more important than what the world dictates.

Sri Ramakrishna explains the role of *purushartha* beautifully, through the example of a cow that has been tied to a post in an open field. The cow is not absolutely free. The rope limits the cow's movement, but it is free to eat the grass in the circle circumscribed by the length of the rope. Only after it has exercised this limited freedom and eaten all the grass within its reach will the owner move it to a different spot. If the cow is dexterous or very hungry, the owner intervenes and extends the rope or ties it at a better spot. *Prarabdha* karma is like the rope that limits our freedom to manifest the potentiality within us. However, we must be active and use *purushartha* to achieve whatever is within our grasp. Only after we have made full and proper use of the freedom that has been given to us through *purushartha*, can we expect our 'rope' or destiny to be extended or changed. So, this parable implies that we can reshape our lives if we persevere and struggle.

We cannot possibly know what kind of *prarabdha* karma we have unless we first try and use *purushartha* to achieve our goals. We should be ready to accept favourable or unfavourable results as the fruit of our *prarabdha* karma, only when we have sincerely put in all possible efforts. This power to discriminate and accept the truth is essential to lead a balanced life and is at the core of learning the Art of Action.

In Conclusion

The theory of karma, *prarabdha* karma in particular, teaches us that though past karma determines an individual's life and its conditions, how we use the given environment depends entirely on us. A man should not be judged by the suffering he undergoes but by his capacity to rise above them. The effects of past karmas were responsible for the terrible suffering that the mighty *Pandavas* of the Mahabharata had to endure. But their virtues, supreme moral strength and the grace of their divine friend Sri Krishna, lifted them above all trials, enabling them to emerge victorious. Their ability to rise above all circumstances by reposing faith in their own strength, in values and in God demonstrated their true character.

Righteousness, the prescribed way of life, brings spiritual joy and peace as its result. A way of life that is not righteous leads to unhappiness, both here and hereafter. Every individual is responsible for his prosperity or adversity, elevation or degradation, enjoyment or suffering. Depending on how we use the freedom of action, we can either elevate or degrade our lives. Dependence on some unknown supernatural power will only weaken us. The Law of Karma lays the whole responsibility on human being and gives it the power to shape its future destiny. Although it is impossible to change *prarabdha*, it is possible to reduce its intensity by sincere prayer, says the Holy Mother. If we are to be hit by a sword, by the grace of God, it may turn out to be a mere pinprick!

Swami Vivekananda said, 'Every thought that we think, every deed that we do, after a certain time becomes fine, goes into seed form, so to speak, and lives in the fine body in a potential form, and after a time it emerges again and bears its results. These results condition the life of man. Thus he moulds his own life. Man is not bound by any other laws excepting those which he makes for himself.'

'Each one of us is the maker of his own fate. This law knocks on the head at once all doctrines of predestination and fate.... we, we, and none else, are responsible for what we suffer. We are the effects and we are the causes. We are free therefore. If I am unhappy, it has been of my own making and that very thing shows that I can be happy if I will. If I am impure, that is also of my own making and that very thing shows that I can be pure if I will. The human will stands beyond all circumstance.'

Summarising the Art of Action, let us therefore decide to lead our lives in such a manner that every action of ours adds to our store of good karma. A time will come when we shall be unable to do anything but good and rise beyond desiring results for our actions. We will be working as masters, with no good or bad karmas to bind us back to this world. Karma is the cause for our birth and if we have to go beyond this cycle and attain everlasting joy, then we have to get rid of the golden chain of good deeds too. When we have mastered this technique, then karma becomes karma yoga, skill in action.

7
Practise! Practise! Practise!

'The mind naturally tends towards evil deeds. It is lethargic in doing good work… That is why I say that perseverance and tenacity are necessary for success in all good works.'
—Holy Mother Sri Sarada Devi

'One ounce of practice is worth a thousand pounds of theory.' 'Practise makes us what we shall be.'
—Swami Vivekananda

In order to manage our lives, it is important to realize that mere intellectual understanding of the principles enumerated here is not enough. What we need is practice. We can achieve the impossible through practice. Arjuna admits his incapability to control the mind, which is as subtle as wind. Sri Krishna assures him that it is possible to gain control over it by practice and renunciation. We need to implement ideas in order to bring about changes in our life. Mere reading and discussing or dreaming about the various possibilities

7

does not help much. Practice makes a man perfect. Genius is one percent inspiration and ninety nine percent perspiration!

Practice is of Greatest Importance

If we examine the lives of great men—scientists, philosophers or sages—we find that the key to their success is in practice. They dedicate themselves to practising their calling with such sincerity and devotion that success is guaranteed in whatever they take up. Even in daily life, practice is essential to be able to achieve anything. For example, a student must practise his lessons in order to pass the exams. In fact, it is through practice that we have mastered the ability to walk and write, so much so that we do not feel the strain any more.

Repeated action creates a habit. We can cultivate good habits through repeated good acts and give up bad habits by using our will-power. Habits influence our mind and nervous systems in such a way that they become a part of our nature, our character. If you want to know a man, study his habits. Once we have formed undesirable habits, then it is very difficult to get over them or change them. Yet, all is not lost. Difficult activities such as swimming, cycling, and so on become easy after regular practice. Similarly, other acts and habits can be modified with practice, patience and perseverance. Many are not aware of the tremendous power of practice.

In fact, even reason is considered subordinate to practice. Through practice we can develop habits that stay with us even in times of great stress or danger, whereas reason can simply desert us at such times. This is why firefighters can successfully save people from a building on fire, while others simply panic. These firefighters are made to practise the procedure so many times that it becomes habitual and they are able to perform involuntarily even when their lives are at risk.

Since our early childhood, we practise writing and doing most of our jobs with the right hand. Suppose there is an accident and the hand is injured, we start doing all the work with the left hand and it becomes natural to us. A man who has been practising tabla for years starts moving his hands as soon as he hears music, automatically, even if he is not sitting in front of the tabla. So powerful is the power of practice.

For a true seeker of peace, practice is of utmost importance. The unfortunate reality is that we are willing to do and continue doing something evil and harmful for two minutes of pleasure, rather than doing something that will benefit us for the rest of our lives. This only shows that we lack proper resolve and will-power to improve ourselves.

Practice Helps Shape Character

Looking within, we find that the real reason for unhappiness is lack of control on our mind. Due to this lack of control, we cannot focus and achieve our goals. The indiscipline and misconduct of our mind induces lack of concentration.

A person who habitually smokes cigarettes every evening is so attuned to this harmful practice that if that person runs out of stock, one does not mind walking ten miles to buy some more! One may be aware that the spectre of lung cancer comes closer with every cigarette smoked, but in spite of being thoroughly exhausted after a hard day's work, one will still walk those ten miles. If only we had this kind of resolve when it comes to developing constructive habits, peace and happiness in our lives!

The danger of wrong practice can be further understood by citing the example of a man who comes from his village to the city in search of work. By misfortune, he befriends a gang of murderers, unknowingly. When he comes to know of their activities, at first he is horrified and disgusted. By this time, through his regular contact with them, his own morals have become so diluted that he is finally ready to kill another for the sake of only one hundred rupees! Association with people of evil tendencies, such as friends who waste their time in loitering, going to the cinema or gossiping, will kill our power to discriminate. To truly transform ourselves, we must immediately cut off all contact with such people, even if it means breaking a friendship of many years.

In the previous chapter we have seen how actions become *samskaras*, which form and mould our personalities, not only in this life but also in future lives. This makes it clear that repeated practice of good actions will result in an abundance of good *samskaras* and hence good character. This will also lead to favourable conditions in future lives. On the contrary, practice of bad habits will give us only unfavourable conditions in the future. If we wish to reform bad conduct or bad habits, then it must be through good conduct and good habits. Such practice will also give us self-confidence and strengthen our mind to such an extent that we will feel peace and joy in spite of adverse external circumstances. Many people tend to brood on their faults and shortcomings, worrying about how they will overcome them. This is an extremely harmful habit and instead of helping us, it saps our energies and makes us relive those negative influences, thereby strengthening them. Instead of worrying about our faults, we should rather focus our energies on methods to avoid them and improve our character.

It is because of a strong character, shaped by years of spiritual practice and deep faith in the divinity of man that great sages are able to radiate peace and joy even in trying circumstances. To develop such character, we need right resolve and perseverance to continue practising. Most people start off with good intentions but after a few days of practice, they get bored or disheartened and give up. However, the same people may practise so hard when they want to get admitted to a reputed college. So, effort depends on our sense of urgency, necessity and utility. None can deny that managing our life and controlling our mind is beneficial. Only, we do not give priority to this and give various reasons to justify our false steps.

Age-old wisdom says that if one takes up practising something noble, it should not be given up—even for a day. The danger is that if we neglect our practice even once, the mind will invent some excuse or the other to skip the practice in future as well. Sri Sarada Devi was down with fever once and she could not get up early in the morning, as was her practice. The next day also she felt like getting up late! She knew the trick her mind was playing and said later, 'the mind must not be given any lenience'.

Miracle of Practice

At times, we feel discouraged because the progress that we are making may not be commensurate with our efforts and practice becomes routine, dull and monotonous after initial enthusiasm ebbs. However, at such times, we should persevere by reminding ourselves of the following facts, to convince ourselves of the efficacy of regular practice.

Think of the amazing feats performed by circus artists. riding a horse standing on one leg, walking on a thin rope that hangs sixty feet above the ground, and so on. How are they able to perform these feats without fear? Practising the same thing over and over again for years together has made them perfect.

Another wonderful example is that of a farmer, who used to carry a bull calf on his shoulders while crossing the river to reach his fields, everyday. He did this month after month and as the calf gradually grew bigger and bigger, the man's capacity to carry the heavy weight also kept developing, till he was able to carry the fully grown bull on his shoulders! This impossible feat was made possible only because of the wonderful power of regular practice.

Waves of the ocean wash against the rocks slowly but surely and wear away the hardest rocks into nothing but tiny particles of sand! Similarly, the repeated rubbing of earthen pots can create a depression in the concrete floor, next to a tube well. Certainly, it is a long process, but the end result is so miraculous! Through repeated friction, the waves and the earthen pots, weak by themselves, change the shape of the stone! Patient efforts pay and this gives us hope.

If you had seen the now famous scientists, during their childhood days, struggling to learn the alphabets, would you have ever thought that they would become so famous? Did Einstein ever think that he would become so great when he was still a small child, learning simple lessons in the class? It is only aspiration and practice that transformed them into great people.

We are not able to improve our lives because we lack earnestness in putting right efforts, a lack of interest in keeping up the practice. This is why we fail in so many of our endeavours. When even wild beasts such as lions and tigers can be trained to perform tricks in a circus, why can we not control our mind? One must have enough patience and perseverance to keep up the practice steadily for a long time. Once it becomes a habit, we will feel uncomfortable even if we miss a single day. The mind will calm down at the stipulated time and we will start deriving an inner joy from our practice. This alone can sustain us and strengthen our resolve to continue.

Knowingly or unknowingly, we all are doing one thing or another at a given time. Some are engaged in acts that ensure successful careers and businesses while some may be busy in ruining themselves by repeatedly indulging in bad activities! We therefore need to consciously discriminate between short-lived pleasures and our life's goals and orient our acts accordingly. There must be no excuse, no compromise and no laxity in this. But what happens if we fail in our attempts, if we err?

The Lord says encouragingly, in the *Bhagavad Gita*, 'With regard to this, there is no waste of the unfinished attempt; nor is there production of contrary results. The practice of even a little of this dharma protects one from great fear.' It is up to us to put in even this small amount of effort so that we can reap the glorious harvest for the rest of our lives.

In the *Bhagavad Gita*, Arjuna asks the Lord, 'How to control the mind which by its very nature is turbulent, obstinate and restless?' Sri Krishna's simple reply is that only practice and non-attachment can help control the mind. If there was any other way, surely the Lord would have told his dear friend and disciple!

8
Developing Will-Power to Achieve True Success

Will-power is the one common factor of success in any work. We may say that studying for an exam requires a different kind of effort than preparing for a hurdle race, but the one key factor in any achievement is will-power. Without this, a student will not be able to motivate himself to study long hours nor will an athlete be prepared to spend long hours training in the sun. The degree of success varies in proportion to will-power. In fact, this is true of any endeavour, even in the field of spiritual development. Without will-power, self-development or improvement is impossible—this is a simple but 100% true fact. In the absence of will-power, all talents, qualities and endeavours come to nothing.

We commit errors and face tragedies in life because we lack will-power. We know what is good for us and will help us progress; yet we are unable to find the strength to pursue such a course of action. We know what is harmful and what we should refrain from, yet we are unable to avoid such actions. For example, a doctor does know the harmful effects of drinking alcohol and smoking. Yet, he cannot give up his addiction to these. Many people repeatedly promise not to continue with these bad habits; but when the temptation comes, they immediately forget everything and get back to square one. It seems that they promise not to drink just to break the promise! The same situation can be seen in the lives of the present day youth who know that watching useless serials on TV, whiling away time in a bandstand, watching profane films and so on will only distract them and scatter their mind, which should be focused on studies. Yet, they cannot bring themselves to follow the advice of their elders and end up confused and lost. Why do we behave in this manner, whether knowingly or unknowingly? The answer is simple, because of lack of will-power.

Someone who has the habit of taking tea at 4 PM everyday will always feel the urge for tea at this time, whether or not tea is placed before him. If in some urgent work, he forces himself to complete the work before enjoying his cup of tea. This is an example of the use of will-power. In fact, developing will-power is nothing but redirecting the already existing power of the will to positive uses.

Defining Will-Power

Will-power itself is a compound of our self (ego) and our mind—it is the positive and creative function of the mind, which impels us along a particular course of action and enables us to do our chosen activities in a definite way. It is the power of the mind, which enables us to do what we know to be right, and to desist from doing what we know to be wrong.

There are a few key points we must keep in mind if we truly wish to develop will-power:

(a) We should have clear understanding that any one, without exception, is capable of increasing the will-power provided they are ready to apply themselves and work towards it steadily and methodically. Have faith in yourself—steady and sincere practise will surely bring along this much wanted fruit of will-power. Swami Vivekananda has said, 'You are the creator of your own destiny. All the strength and succour you want is within yourself.' What a life-giving, saving message he has given us! He has made it so simple for us—all we need to do is place faith in his words and grow steadily.

(b) For many of us the problem is that we do not will or desire to improve will-power. We feel that we are weak and helpless and so can never improve. Remember Swamiji's message quoted above and know for certain that within each one of us is infinite, unlimited power. This doubt or delusion about our own capabilities must be firmly removed—otherwise this doubt will weaken our resolve and we will be incapable of developing ourselves.

(c) An important prerequisite to developing will-power is removing the dichotomy between the head and the heart, the intellect and emotion, between thinking and feelings. We may intellectually resolve to undertake a particular task or work towards achieving a goal, but unless we have true love for the goal or deep-seated desire to attain it, our resolve will never last long enough for us to be successful. Without this, any resolve we undertake will remain on our lips and will not penetrate into the innermost core of our heart. The way out is to cultivate true love for the divine. This need not be interpreted to mean that we must love some particular god, but simply that we should worship our own divinity, our own infinite strength hidden within. Assert the divine within; the devil will run out on its own. In this, we must stand tall like heroes and struggle till victory is ours. It is of no avail to weep and cry that we are weak and helpless. Success that comes without struggle has no meaning. The problem is that we do not have enough love for the ideal. If we really love the ideal then all doubts and diffidence will vanish.

(d) Two major enemies of will-power are, (i) our regrets about the past, and (ii) our worries about the future. It is immensely better to live in the present than to wallow in the past or worry about the future. In any case, we cannot change the past, nor is brooding going to help us change the future. On the other hand, if we focus on the present, we can build our character to improve our future. Many times we brood on our past mistakes with the idea that we are repenting them. Actually, the truth is that there is very little regret in such an action; mostly we are mentally enjoying the same actions over and over again under the cover of righteous regret. To escape all thoughts of the past and worries about the future, you must think that you are free, not bound. You must remember you are not this insignificant body, which is subject to disease, decay and death. You are, instead, the infinite Atman and pure, infinite bliss is your true nature. Learn to live a wakeful life in the living present.

(e) To live in the present, we require the guidance of a sound sense of values—physical, mental, and verbal. These values enable us to live in the present and prevent external events from disturbing our peace of mind. People without values are constantly tossed around by their own ever changing desires and by pressures of the external world. It is values that provide an anchor to life.

(f) We need to constantly discriminate between what is real and what is unreal. We spend our whole lives wanting peace of mind and imagine that we can get this through money and possessions. Ultimately, everyone who follows this foolish path ends up broken and disheartened. We can attain peace only if we have a pure and calm mind and only if we live a virtuous life. Money and other material possessions have never helped anyone gain peace, nor will they ever do so in the future. Peace is an attribute of God that you can attain only through virtue and by no other means.

(g) We must keep ourselves busy at all times. Idle curiosity about others' affairs will not only get us into trouble; it will also ruin our mental peace. An unoc-cupied mind tends to indulge in all sorts of foolish pastimes and fantasies. Those who have a task at hand such as studying for an exam should do so with all sincerity, instead of wasting time. One can pursue a hobby to keep the mind occupied during free time. Naturally the mind dislikes such control and wants to wander free and unrestricted. However, discipline is a must if we really wish to change. Bringing up children and disciplining them is not the hardest task in the world! But disciplining our own selves is!

(h) You must stop all squandering of mental energy through useless talks, purposeless work, futile contro-versies, daydreaming and so on. You can channel en-ergy saved by refraining from these pursuits to pursue constructive activities. Many people exhaust not only themselves, but all around them by their constant tsu-nami of words. What do they gain in the end? Nothing but reproaches from others and lack of peace within. Hence, conserve your energy and focus on improving your life, rather than on idle gossip.

(i) Conserve your physical energy by living a moral life. Often it is seen that modern youths squander away their precious mental and physical vitality by indulg-ing in harmful activities and habits such as smoking or drinking or even obsession with ideas and ideals expressed in serials and movies. Such people generally end up as utter failures in life and even if they achieve some amount of material success, they are found to be lacking in peace and serenity without which life is a constant burden.

(j) Failure should be accepted as a part of the game of life. Many times, when faced with failure, people tend to get broken-hearted and lose all enthusiasm for further efforts. We should instead live life as a game and accept whatever success or failure comes our way, as a part of the game. We need not get too excited by success, or too depressed by failure.

Using the above precepts, we must root out all that is evil and cultivate all that is good within us. We must give the will an appropriate direction. One may develop a strong will but unless inner purity exists, such a will can be misused to bring misery to oneself and others. For example, Hitler certainly had a very strong will, but how many would claim that such a will brought any good to the world? In the end, all that Hitler managed to achieve was the death and destruction of many lives all over the world and he himself died in the most wretched condition.

Understanding the Importance of Discipline

Any attempt to develop will-power shall fail unless we develop discipline along with it. Every student knows what he or she must do to pass the exams. Yet, only those who have the habit of setting aside a few hours everyday to study and revise their lessons can make any progress. Students who lack this discipline may be very brilliant, but they will still not fare well in the exams.

Trying to improve life through various methods, but completely ignoring the essential point of discipline, serves no purpose. Getting up at whatever time one likes, skipping breakfast, having lunch at 1 PM on one day and at 3 PM on another, such pattern of behaviour is indicative of indiscipline and irregularity. Such a mind will be unfocused and unable to achieve anything. How then can the person expect to change his or her personality?

To reform, try and follow to the extent possible, some sort of timetable in life. For instance, practise waking up at a particular time everyday. This simple routine will induce the mind to obey at other times too. In fact, if you look at the lives of people who have achieved great things in life—whether in the spiritual domain or in the material domain, you find that all of them have tremendous personal discipline.

Sri Sarada Devi, who is considered the spiritual mother of the entire Ramakrishna Movement, had tremendous discipline, which would inspire all those who were acquainted with her. She was in the habit of waking up at 3 AM everyday. One day, being ill, she woke up a little later. Even on the next day, although she was cured, the mind felt lethargic and was inducing her to wake later. She knew the trick the mind was playing. Her disciplined life gave her the power and alertness to detect and correct this behaviour immediately.

It is said that discipline is one of the better methods towards self-development. Of course, some patience is needed, but depending on our sincerity, positive changes can be seen in a matter of days. It is a proven fact that sleep of more than six hours is not required; we feel the need to sleep longer because the mind is tricking us. If you truly wish to be a master of your life, you must assert authority over the mind. Bring in a little respect for time in your life and see what a wonderful difference it makes.

Understanding the Powers of the Mind

The mind has different powers—reason, volition (exercise of will) and emotion.

(a) Emotion is the capacity for feeling. There are emotions that attract us, such as kindness, charity, love, and so on and there are emotions that repel us such as hatred, anger, jealousy, fear, and the like.

(b) Volition is associated with decision-making. It is the ability that every human has, to choose one path from many options. For instance, I may ask you to leave the room—it is your decision whether to obey or not. Of course, your decision may or may not be right from a moral standpoint, but still the freedom to choose is entirely yours. Whenever you exercise your will, you come to a decision and act.

(c) Finally, reason is the power to think cogently. Reason enables us to distinguish between right and wrong, between the real and unreal, between temporal and eternal, good and bad.

Understanding the Role of Reason and Volition in Guiding Emotions

Volition and emotion must be under the guidance of reason, but emotion should be controlled by volition. One may be able to reason and find the right path, and having decided on it, he or she must further have the ability to go forward on that path. However, due to some wrong emotion, we may give in to temptation and not act appropriately. Here, emotion stands in the way and will-power is not strong enough to control emotion. For example, knowing very well the impact of seeing a movie or a bad serial, we continue to do so because our will-power is not strong enough to foil the plan of emotion. If a master exploits his servant to bring illicit drugs and both enjoy the same, then eventually the servant will not obey his master. Similarly we utilise our will-power in wrong things and instead of being our slave, the mind is lording over us—we are constantly subject to its many whims and fancies.

Everybody knows the method to success in life. Why then do so many fail? The philosophy and way of living to achieve happiness, as elucidated in all the scriptures, is so simple and so convincing to the rational human intellect that one wonders why only a few people attain perfection. The honest answer is utterly simple. All living creatures follow their own tendencies (*vasanas*) and act as they think.

The source of all activity in every creature is thus its tendencies or *vasanas*. Even an erudite scholar, who has intellectually understood the technique follows his tendencies and fails to live it. Why? Beings follow their own nature. A lawyer, who knows law, may under provocation, even commit murder. What we know is not sufficient for us; we need to live what we know. Intellectually we may applaud and appreciate certain moral values of life, but act as lowly as though we have no education at all. Strange is the paradox. Just because I appreciate music or painting, it does not mean that I can sing and paint. Similarly, we may appreciate that knowledge is important, but to implement this knowledge we need a lot of mental strength, inclination to become better and will-power. An educated person may behave worse than an uneducated person. The educated man has worldly knowledge which gives him power over nature and fellow human beings, but he lacks culture, the training of mind that gives him the ethical ability to use that power for the mutual benefit of himself and the society. Man has to conquer his lower selfish nature and progress by utilizing the power of the higher nature of the Self that is within him.

Mere Academic Knowledge is Not Enough

A morose man returns home from work, tired. His wife brings him his customary cup of coffee but no sooner does he sip it, he howls and roars; cursing and complaining that there is no sugar in the coffee. His loving wife calls out from the kitchen that she has added the sugar in the cup. But this only further enrages the man. She then calls out and tells that the spoon is in the saucer. Still murmuring and complaining about his fate, the man stirs his coffee and lifts the cup to his lips. As soon as he sips the coffee, all complaints stop. In silence he drinks his coffee and goes out. The wife simply smiles knowingly. Just as the cup of coffee had sugar, the erudite scholar had knowledge. But the coffee was not stirred properly, and so was not sweet. When book knowledge is well digested with reflection and practice for some time, then knowledge can come to our help. Otherwise, like the erudite scholar we will simply live like bookworms. Instruction is objective and education is subjective. We have many instructional institutes but no educational schools. We have many instructors, but hardly any teachers in this modern age. Real teachers can, by their example and nobility, help to maintain the inspiration kindled in the student.

Renunciation of Desire Essential for Peace

Before we commit a mistake, we know very well what is right and what is wrong. After the incident, we regret the compromise we made during the incident. Why is it that at the actual moment of committing the wrong act we do not hesitate? In spite of knowing everything, we are guilty of regrettable acts of violence, of indecency, of immorality, of corruption, of falsehood. Why is this so? What is this dark force that compels us to indulge in such deeds even though in our saner moments we do not want to commit them? The answer is so plain, straight, direct and clear. It is the *vasana*—or inborn tendencies born of past actions. We have indulged in evil acts repeatedly, and this now becomes part and parcel of our nature. This is true whether we are discussing the urge towards lust or towards anger. All human beings have these urges of lust and anger in them. The goal is to use one's intellect to overcome these urges.

Nature has given man freedom to utilize his powers judiciously, whereas animals have no freedom but can only obey the lower instincts. In fact, as an animal stands on its four legs, its head, heart, belly and lower portions are all in one horizontal line—signifying perhaps equal importance. But man has learnt to stand on his two legs, in an erect position. In his case, the order of precedence is head, heart, belly and then finally the sex organs. The head is highest and sex organs the lowest. Therefore, man is expected to live as his head or intellect guides him. But today our youth seem to consider sex as the *summum bonum* of life and the result of such a philosophy can easily be seen in the crisis facing all sections of society. One who wants to control his passions must utilise his brain properly; else he is no better than an animal—perhaps a little more intelligent, that is all!

As a flame is covered by smoke, a mirror by dust and a foetus by the womb, so is knowledge covered by desire (especially lust)—so say our ancient and time-tested scriptures. It is lust that dims the mirror of knowledge within us and causes so much misery and unhappiness. Lust has its headquarters at three main centres – in the sense organs, in the mind, and in the intellect. We need discriminative knowledge or wisdom to foil the plan of lust. There is a story that runs as follows: A gang of thieves reaches a house where a party is going on. At a precise moment, one thief cuts off the electric power. In the resulting confusion, another snatches the priceless jewels worn by the guests and throws them out of the window. Another thief waiting outside the window catches them safely. There is much screaming and shouting, and in panic, all guests run for the door. Then suddenly the light comes on and all the ladies mourn their losses. Here lust is the thief that veils the light of wisdom in us and in the resulting darkness, the sense organs, mind, and intellect act wildly. The loss is of the necklace of peace and the diamond pendant of joy.

We see an object of desire and the sense organs are tempted; the feeling of desire then rises in our mind. The more we contemplate, the more powerful our desires become. So, sense organs are the grossest and controlling them is naturally easiest. If we refuse to see exciting images, then naturally the thoughts associated with such images will be lesser and consequently our task of controlling the mind will be easier. Lust cannot delude us if we are alert. It is only when we are relaxed and careless that desires or lust overpower us and, inadvertently, we become slaves to it.

There is another amusing story that illustrates our point more clearly. An Indian was touring America for a while and made an American friend. One day, when the American had to come to India for some work, his friend told him to eat the famous '*elaichi*' banana of Mumbai. At his hotel, the American tried to eat the banana, but contrary to his friend's claims, he disliked the fruit immensely! A little later he visited the Indian at his home and when his friend asked him how he liked the banana, the American heaped abuses on him and said that he had never tasted anything as foul as that wretched banana! Not believing him, the Indian called his daughter and told her to offer the American another *elaichi* banana. But when the American started eating it, the Indian burst out laughing because he saw his friend eat the fruit without peeling it! When the American saw his mistake and ate the fruit properly, naturally he found it to be very good indeed. Now this short story highlights the wretchedness of our life. The pulp of banana in this story stands for peace and the skin stands for attachment and desire. We attempt to gain peace without removing our attachments and desires. So, we suffer every minute of our lives. It is a fool's dream to cling on to low material attachments and desires and still want a peaceful life. Never has a person succeeded in finding happiness in the material world before and never shall such a thing occur in the future as well.

Those who sincerely want peace must give up their attachments, at least to the extent possible. Our scriptures say, '*tyagenaike amritatvamanashuh*', meaning, only through renunciation of desire, immortality can be attained. We waste many years chasing desires and accumulating money, possessions, children, status, and what not. Still peace has only receded from our lives. In truth, peace is directly proportional to our level of renunciation. The more we give up, the happier we are. This is why we see sages who have renounced all as the happiest, most peaceful people on earth. Of course, as discussed earlier, man has the choice to follow whatever path he likes. If you wish to burn, then who can save you? If you wish to reform, then no power in the universe can stop you.

Understanding the Importance of Attitude

It should be clear from all our discussion so far that merely memorising points will never help. First, there must be discipline in our lives, and second, we must have the right attitude to wait patiently for changes to manifest themselves. Some would even say that discipline and attitude is one and the same thing. A change of attitude involves disciplining the mind's response to the outside world. A man may find a baby's cries very irritating, but when his own child is born, that same sound is more attractive to him than any music! How to explain this sudden and dramatic transformation? Simply because the love he has for his child has disciplined his mind to some extent and now his attitude towards babies has changed.

Someone has said that although there are various solutions to problems in life, we can gauge their relative effectiveness through the following simple test. First, number all the letters from A to Z as 1 to 26. Then, let us take various solutions and apply a score on them. You may say 'hard work' is an effective solution to any problem. Well, after adding the score of all the letters (h=8 + a=1 and so on), 'hard work'=98. Similarly, knowledge=96, love=54, luck=47, money=72 and so on. But 'attitude'? Attitude=100! So here we have the perfect solution to any problem in life! Change your attitude and see what a joyous, wonderful world you live in!

Be aware, wake up and live—do not sleep at the steering wheel of life's vehicle. You must have a higher ideal. Only then can you lift your mind from a lower level to a higher level. You cannot solve your problem as long as you are part of the problem. The problem of poverty is solved only when you grow rich, war ends only when peace comes, illness ends only when health returns. So the problem of sense organs and mind ends only when we identify ourselves with the Self within.

Part II

Conflict Management

9
The Cause of Human Suffering

'One suffers as a result of one's own actions. So, instead of blaming others for such suffering, one should pray to the Lord and depending entirely on His grace, try to bear them patiently with forbearance under all circumstances.'

'One must be patient like the earth. What iniquities are being perpetrated on her! Yet she quietly endures them all. Man, too, should be like that.

—Holy Mother Sri Sarada Devi

It is possible to categorise human suffering into three broad categories, based on the type of conflicts an individual encounters during the course of his life.

Conflicts between Man and Nature occur due to external factors that are unavoidable, accidental, or uncontrollable, such as earthquakes, hot weather, floods, tsunami, and the like. Life is never the same for those who survive the fury of nature's wrath! Widespread deaths, separation from loved ones, and loss of livelihood cause physical and mental trauma, which continue to haunt them for the rest of their lives.

Conflicts between Man and Man happen due to disagreements, disharmony, and other differences amongst fellow humans, resulting in wars, family turmoil, riots, theft, and so on. It also includes the suffering caused by other creatures, such as a snake or a dog through their bites.

Conflicts within Man caused by anger, jealousy, stress, fear, guilt, and other such emotional upheavals result in depression, feeling of worthlessness, suicidal tendency, and so on.

We have little or no control over the first category. We can avoid external conflicts with other beings by following precautionary measures and by mutual understanding. Prevention as well as cure for the last kind is entirely in the hands of the individual, it is an internal struggle. If this is achieved, it automatically helps us in overcoming the first two categories of suffering also! The first part of the book has already looked into some of the causes of conflicts within man. The second part now details some practical tips, which can lessen our suffering.

Anger, jealousy, and improper use of our sense organs like the eyes and ears are some of the causes of our suffering. These are therefore treated separately in the following chapters of this part of the book.

We Suffer Because we Look at Life as a Fight Instead of a Game

While the succeeding chapter discusses this in detail, it is sufficient to say here that just as in any other sport, for success in the game of life, we need to be well conversant with its rules, regulations, instruments, customs, and etiquettes.

We Suffer Due to Unfulfilled Desires

In the preceding chapters we have discussed the cause for restlessness in life, which may persist in spite of many of our desires being fulfilled. With every achievement we assume that have attained everlasting peace and happiness. Sooner or later this peace wanes and we are left stranded as before. The lacuna within makes us seek happiness without. Hoping to attain peace through fulfilment of desires is like trying to put out a flame by pouring butter on it! The fulfilment of a long cherished desire gives rise to further new desires. For instance, moving into our new dream house does not really provide the happiness that we hoped for. Instead, new desires to furnish and paint it to our liking will destroy whatever peace we may have had. Or, possessing a brand new car will again preoccupy our mind with thoughts of the upholstery, music system, suitable parking space, and maintenance.

There are numerous such desires of varying intensities that either remain unfulfilled or somehow get fulfilled, but not entirely to our satisfaction. Our mind gets scattered in different directions as we pursue such frivolous desires causing anger, jealousy, frustration, stress, and so on. Thus trying to fulfil desires not only fails to rid us of suffering, it instead results in more suffering!

As long as our desires are subservient to the main goal in life, they will not hinder our progress. A bird needs to streamline all its energies to fly efficiently. Similarly we must learn to eliminate unwanted desires by constant discrimination and remain focused. Desiring occasionally is not as bad as desiring everything that one sees! Life is too valuable to be wasted in useless pursuits.

We Suffer as we are Attached to Possessions and Loved Ones

A woman suffers immensely at the loss of her own young son; however, when her nephew dies a few days later, her suffering is not as intense. She is unfortunate to face two tragedies, but in two different roles, for her attachment as a mother is far stronger than her attachment as an aunt. This explains the difference in the intensity of her grief. Thus the intensity of suffering depends upon the intensity of attachment.

It is the same with our other possessions too. A small scratch on the car's door caused by a passing cyclist is inevitable in a city's chaotic traffic conditions. It may be of no consequence to others, but it is enough to lacerate the heart of a man who is so fondly attached to his dream-machine!

Concern for the well-being and safety of our kith and kin or of our possessions in itself is worrisome enough. To add to this, we are pained by the indifferent and uncaring or ungrateful attitude of people we love; their misbehaviour towards us in spite of our well-meaning intentions. All of this can drive even the most educated and cultured amongst us to lose poise and become mad in anguish.

It is a common refrain among people that material assets and close relatives are the prime source of their suffering. They do not mean what they say for they are not yet ready to live without these strong attachments. We need to learn to detach ourselves from others and from objects because these attachments bind us more and more to the world, to our limited body and mind. This may be hard to achieve, but when we succeed, we will be able to feel free—no longer depending on something or somebody for our existence. Relatives, after all are just 'relative'—they are not absolute. Our relationship with these people, in our lifetime, is like the relationship we share with co-passengers on a train journey. Sooner or later, we must part ways, and each one of us will have to proceed alone to the ultimate goal.

We Suffer Because we do not Consider our Suffering as Blessings in Disguise

A woman willingly undergoes the suffering of child birth with the hope of seeing her child and caring for it. Although a natural urge, she finds fulfilment in being a mother and does not despise the suffering.

A young lad completely disregards the concerns of his doting parents and is engrossed in playing football with his friends on a hot Sunday afternoon. The joy of playing in the company of his friends is superior to his parents' ire, the discomfort of sweat under the burning sun, and the sheer exhaustion that will eventually follow. Suffering has become joyous here!

Yet there are times when we refuse to accept our suffering. People turn bitter, cold-hearted and suffer bouts of depression and start asking, 'Why me?' Marriages ending in divorce and failing to get a good job, or a promotion are often causes for blaming those around us. The common complaint in any unfavourable situation is, 'What have I done to get this sort of treatment?' Ordinarily, people complain, fret and fume, mourn their losses for some time and then, they are back to their old ways. A student who fails in his exams swears, 'I'll never watch television. I will completely ignore the temptation of movies and stop hanging around with friends. I will not bother about their taunts of not enjoying life.' However, within a month he is back to his old tricks of missing tuition and playing in the fields with his friends!

Adversities can bring about a change for the better in some, if they are mature and open to reason. Although aged, the grief of losing his dear wife was unbearable for Gopal Chandra Ghosh. Looking for solace he came to Sri Ramakrishna. He realized that death was inevitable, and on being blessed by the saint, blossomed into Swami Advaitananda. The loss of a gold watch caused young Sarada Prasanna prolonged agony and he too came to Sri Ramakrishna seeking peace. The saint opened a higher dimension for him and he transformed into the great disciple, Swami Trigunatitananda. The young prince Siddhartha renounced the life of royal comfort and riches when he saw a dead body ready for funeral, a person suffering from old age and another crippled due to some disease. Introspection on the cause of suffering made him Gautam Buddha and his teachings have continued to help millions of people get rid of their miseries, all over the world, for centuries.

Suffering is a great teacher, imparting wisdom and strength to us. In this regard it is even more powerful than success. It is truly a blessing in disguise. Life's pains, trials, and tribulations have an immensely beneficial impact on the thoughts and emotions of the concerned person, only if he or she accepts them in the right spirit. Cursing our fate only worsens the situation. Swami Vivekananda says that misery is a greater teacher and man has to train in this moral gymnasium called life, through its ups and downs.

We Suffer Because we Fail to Understand that the World Does Not Move as per Our Wishes

We normally expect everybody and everything around us to be as we want it to be. That cannot and does not always happen! There will invariably be times when we are forced to adjust, and failure to do so results in suffering.

For instance, we must not expect that everyone will be polite to us. Just because someone happens to be rude to us, we should not spoil our mood for the day. We need to gradually accept that life doles out many such bitter fruits over which we have little or no control. Of course, this does not mean that we should allow people to take advantage of our good nature. When someone tries to take undue advantage of us, it is important to tell him in a calm and dignified manner that such behaviour is unacceptable.

A long cherished desire of ours may remain unfulfilled due to a sudden development over which we have little control. For instance, a person, repeatedly told by the office management that he is one of the most eligible and deserving candidates for promotion, may be denied the post because it surprisingly tilted in favour of an inexperienced colleague who was just about to marry the daughter of the boss! His unique qualification got consideration over other factors! What options does the person who lost have? Should he shout and scream, taking recourse to legal action or should he calmly accept it as an outcome of his karma? It is the duty of the individual to fight injustice of any kind. If legal option is not possible, he can opt for another job based on his work experience. If he decides to fight back, he must think calmly, consult legal experts and above all must take care to avoid unethical means.

Even Arjuna, the great warrior of the Mahabharata was faced with a difficult choice: to escape from the battlefield and avoid the inevitable war or to gird up his loins and prepare for a battle in which he would have to kill his own kinsmen, including his beloved grandfather, Bhishma.

We Suffer When we Compare Ourselves to Others and are Unhappy to See Others Achieve

A young man gets selected to a prestigious college and celebrates heartily with all his friends. But the moment he comes to know that his rival classmate has been selected for an even better college, his exuberant mood suddenly turns sullen. Jealousy makes him lose interest in his own achievement and instead of focusing on what he has got, his entire focus shifts to what the other person has got. Instead of such negative feelings, we must learn to rejoice at other's success.

To concentrate on our goal and the means of achieving it does not mean that we must compete and deny others their rights. All progress must be based on values and an individual must learn to be content with his own achievements.

We Suffer Because we Cannot Distinguish Between Education and Knowledge

We often use the words education and knowledge interchangeably, but these two words mean very different things. Education means schooling which imparts certain skills to help us live in this world. It is the collection of data while knowledge means the discovery of truth. Knowledge cannot be imparted, but education can be imparted. We can teach a child to read and write but we cannot give it knowledge, perception, or insight into the true nature of a thing. A child can be taught the rules of grammar and the alphabet but you cannot teach him a comprehensive understanding of the language itself. Many of us know the general rules of grammar involving nouns, verbs, and so on but we do not really know the language. If we are asked to write a poem in our mother tongue, most of us would struggle to put out even one stanza. Some of the greatest poets and writers had no formal education, but their compositions are immortal and heralded by all, including learned professors of language! Education, therefore, must lead to knowledge or the path of discovery and then only will it have served its purpose and be complete.

The present day educational system prepares the mind for a good career but does not prepare the person to live life completely. The typical student has no ideal or goal in his life; he is merely drifting. What will he do with the degree or the education that he receives? He will pursue a job for the sake of money and power. When there is no ideal, there is no further progress or development of character.

This can be vividly seen from the following example. If your ideal in life is to feed others before feeding yourself, then you will do just that. If you lower your ideal, then you may eat without feeding another and if you lower the ideal still further, then you not only eat your own food but the food of others as well. As your ideal falls, so does your behaviour. The vision of the ideal should be the guideline for one's life and true education must play a role in determining that ideal.

Today, however, higher goals are not articulated in the universities; professors concentrate on bookish knowledge and focus only on facts and figures. Consequently, students have education but no knowledge or understanding. Someone asked Swami Chinmay-anandaji, 'I have read the Bhagavad Gita, but nothing has happened.' Swamiji replied, 'You have gone through the Bhagavad Gita, but has the Bhagavad Gita gone through you?' The tragedy of our lives and indeed of modern times is that in spite of so much education, our lives have not changed; we are still the same.

Shankaracharya says that the result of knowledge is the elimination of falsehood. This implies that if I understand something as false, I withdraw myself from it. When my wrong concept clears, the associated wrong conduct automatically corrects. We can use an example to understand. A person sees a piece of rope in the dark and mistakes it for a snake. As a result, he gets terribly frightened and starts screaming, sweating, and so on. However, if another man comes with a lantern and shows him that it is only a rope, immediately all fears vanish and he laughs at his own mistake, with relief.

The moment true knowledge dawned, his ignorance was eliminated. Knowledge removed his fear. Similarly when we wake up to true knowledge, all our suffering come to an end and we become transformed and enlightened persons. True education must give us an insight into our true nature, thereby instilling faith and courage to face the myriad problems of the world.

We have to wake up from three illusions that are the source of all our problems. They are:

We think of ourselves as the physical body

Actually we are not this physical body but the eternal soul or Atman. Our body acts and our mind thinks because of the power of the Atman. This idea must always be kept uppermost in the mind, as it will enable us to remain strong and pure even in the most adverse circumstances.

Money can give me security

This idea is fallacious, for even after procuring money, it certainly cannot remove fear. On the contrary it can be easily seen that the more money one has, the more fear he has about retaining it. One cannot buy happiness and peace. It is a state of being. You cannot possess it.

More sense pleasures bring more happiness

Suppose you sit to eat your favourite food and just then receive the news that a close relative has died. Can you continue to eat and derive sense pleasure as earlier? As discussed earlier, it is the mind that determines the degree of happiness or sorrow.

A small story will help illustrate this point. Once, a certain king was very sick. Many doctors treated him in vain. At last, one of them said that if he were to wear the shirt of a happy man, his illness would vanish. Hearing this, the king's minister approached many wealthy men but they all said that they were not really happy in spite of their riches. At last he came to a man who was sitting beside a river. The man had a blissful smile on his face and upon inquiry the minister discovered that this man was indeed truly happy. When he was asked to give his shirt, the happy man smiled and said that he had no possessions at all, not even a shirt! The great man made the minister realize that happiness was not in the shirt but in the awakened mind. The king was not suffering from a physical malady. He had the erroneous notion that possessions could make him happy.

Knowledge eliminates all false concepts and thereby helps us withdraw from wrong ways of living. Oneness of existence is the highest knowledge. While we may feel that we are separate from others around us, our scriptures and the experiences of mystics affirm that in reality, we are all parts of one whole. This recognition of oneness in diversity is the ultimate or the highest knowledge. For example, our body has many different parts—hands, fingers, stomach, head, legs, eyes, and so on. But I know that these are parts of one body system—namely my own. If someone touches my back, I will not ask, 'Why are you touching my back?' I will ask, 'Why are you touching me?' Each part of my body, however insignificant, has a definite role to play in the body. This higher knowledge can transform us. If I see myself and others as parts of one whole, then love and service for all becomes meaningful and spontaneous—just as my love for my finger remains the same even if it accidentally pokes my eye.

In our present condition we are not able to serve, not because there is no love, but because we have no sense of oneness. If a person has this vision of oneness of all existence, he can change the world around him. The wise man hates none and is a friend of all. What the wise man does after realization can become our practise. Let us try to feel one with everybody. Do not wait for others to change, begin with yourself.

We Suffer Because we Seek Peace Outside

No one can give you peace, but at least a piece of advice can be given! As discussed in previous chapters, all want peace and are struggling to achieve it in some way or the other. We experience a little of this peace now and then in our lives. If it were not so, life would have been miserable. Before we enjoy something, there is a lot of excitement born of expectation and agitation because the pleasure may be lost. At the actual moment of pleasure, we identify ourselves with the object and for a moment there is experience of oneness. We are closest to the Atman at that moment, as the enjoyer, but it is for such a brief moment that soon we are taken over by some other desire. The veil of ignorance still hangs over us. For some time the mind becomes quiet and we experience relative peace, until another agitation starts. This is somewhat like the peace after a riot. When a riot takes place in a city and the police crush it, we say that an uneasy calm prevails. That fragile peace may shatter at any moment.

Religious people dutifully go to temples, mosques and churches to pray, chant and sing the glories of the Lord, or hear spiritual discourses. This gives them some satisfaction and peace. But if this peace has to remain, religion must enter our blood, and we must live religion.

Why does this peace leave us? Because we are seeking it outside like any other object. Peace does not come from anything external. We should realize this first. We have to discover the peace within. Peace is our real nature.

Usually due to restlessness of mind, people live on sensations—newspapers, novels, movies, and so on. While seeking sensations, peace eludes them. It remains hidden behind the whirl of their daily activities. As a result, agitation and restlessness trouble them.

A thousand waves may rise and fall in the ocean, but still the ocean stays as it is. Similarly, peace is always present, but we ourselves create the causes of disturbance, agitation, distraction, and restlessness and lose that peace. If we learn to dive deep within ourselves rather than stay amidst the tumultuous waves on the surface, we shall remain calm and peaceful.

There are four main sources of disturbances: (a) desire (b) attachment (c) I-ness and (d) my-ness. We must strive to give up these four as they disturb us and destroy our peace.

The effects of desire and attachment have already been discussed and here the focus is on the feeling of I-ness and my-ness, which are also causes of sorrow. I-ness refers to our ego. We not only identify ourselves with our body but also extend it to include our possessions, relatives, friends and what not! All these accretions weaken us. Our true blissful self must be realized and asserted if we want lasting peace and joy. Suppose I own a watch and happen to lose it—would this make you unhappy? Of course not, but I would be miserable! But, suppose I gift my watch to somebody and then it is lost—I will not be unhappy as before because, the sense of my-ness is no longer with me. As long as there is this sense of my-ness, the sense of possession, the mind suffers.

The Gita advises us to live in a spirit of *nirmamatva*— or freedom from the sense of my-ness. How can we live without a sense of my-ness? Suppose I have a watch. Whose watch is it? I cannot say, 'I do not know' simply because the Gita advises *nirmamatva*. I would be impelled to say, 'It is mine.' There is no harm in saying this if we understand that possessions are only in our temporary keeping. People feel that they are lost if their possessions are lost! Their very existence depends on these objects! Yet they carry nothing with them when they leave this world, nor did they bring these at the time of birth!

While travelling by train or airplane, if the seat number 15F is allotted, I do not try to take the seat with me when I get off the plane. I accept it as mine only during the time of travel. I relinquish it without a thought, without even looking back, when I leave the plane. I do not consider it as absolutely mine. In the same way, we can live in this world with people and relatives and all the objects, without clinging to them.

We Suffer Because we Do Not Understand the True Meaning of Success

Success is a most fascinating word—the desire to be successful is common with all and it makes man accomplish the impossible! But mostly we do not care to see what truly constitutes meaningful success.

In general parlance, success means material success, to get the desired result of any work undertaken with a purpose. For example, a student appearing in an examination passes with the desired marks and is then considered successful. But as we shall see, material success, such as that enjoyed by a 'successful' doctor or businessman, does not guarantee true success in life.

One psychiatrist said to a monk, 'Swamiji, I have treated many patients and most of them have benefited from my treatment, but I fail to understand the psychology of my people at home.' A brigadier once said, 'I can command the whole brigade, but I cannot say a word to my wife and child.' These people are successful in their professions, but in their domestic lives they have no sense of success. Success in life means the ability to overcome all kinds of problems—problems related to the family, health or finance. The persons mentioned here are experts in handling some problems but are incompetent when it comes to facing life as a whole—such indeed is the case with most of us.

It is true that all successes are not glorified—a murderer, gangster, smuggler, or black marketeer may succeed in his attempts, but we never glorify their successes. Such work is always done on the sly and is always accompanied by fear. Apart from this, such acts harm the social fabric. Sometimes we find persons pursuing a noble path or following a righteous path failing miserably, while on the other hand a corrupt person or a person following an unrighteous path achieves many things. This is a common occurrence in society. Even so, we glorify the failure of the righteous person. Success on the evil path is never glorified. Thus failure on the righteous path is nobler than success on the path of evil. It is important that the means adopted to achieve something be noble. For instance, so many of our freedom fighters like Subhash Chandra Bose, died in their struggles. We still glorify them and sing their praises, appreciating their sacrifices rather than counting their failures, if any.

We must not get infatuated or fascinated by apparent success. Success must bring enhancement of personality, purification of mind, joy, and happiness in life. We are the best judges of all our actions. The world may praise us, but we can never cheat our conscience. We need to balance external achievements with inner growth to develop a successful personality.

Nowadays there are many courses on management, such as effective communication, science of management, and so on. Each of these deals with only one particular aspect of success. That is the whole mistake. We divide life into many small compartments and try to live it in this piecemeal fashion. Merely accomplishing a task that we undertake cannot be the definition of success. Following the path of righteousness which is beneficial to the individual and the society, and attaining the end with peace of mind and happiness that is born of a sense of contentment in life can be termed as success; success that truly makes us strong and powerful.

The succeeding chapters provide some useful insights on how best to reduce our mental suffering.

10
Live Life in the Spirit of a Game

'What an illusion Mahamaya has conjured up! Here is this infinite world and what one claims as his possessions will be left behind at death. Still men cannot understand this simple truth.'—Holy Mother Sri Sarada Devi

What distinguishes a game from a conflict? To understand, let us consider for example the features of a wrestling match and a street fight. Both involve much pushing and jostling, and in both, the opponents try their best to outwit and outplay the other—but the similarity is only external.

Wrestling has certain rules, regulations, and etiquettes to ensure fair play and equal opportunities for all competitors. Although there is stiff competition, generally there is an absence of hatred or enmity. Opponents appreciate and respect each other's strengths. After a match, the loser congratulates the winner. Strangers, playing against each other in a match, often end up as friends for life. Close friends may fiercely oppose each other on the court or on the field, but only during the competition. Feelings of jealousy and bitterness among opponents crop up only when the opponents are obsessed about winning.

A street fight is a free-for-all, where opponents who may have been close friends earlier end up as sworn enemies and fight each other. There is no sportsmanship during such fights. All possible means, fair or foul are used to crush each other. When carried to the extreme, they result in communal clashes and war.

Every human experience may be likened to a match in the game of life wherein there are at least two entities. One is the individual who undergoes the experience. The other is the object of experience, which is external; comprising people, animals, trees, inanimate objects, and so on.

If our interaction with the object of experience is harmonious, we are happy, light-hearted, and radiate goodwill towards others. In such a scenario, people or things around us do not easily irritate us. Our behaviour will be sweet and polite. And whatever the external circumstances, we tend to remain calm and radiate the same outwards. When the interaction is non-harmonious, feelings of enmity, conflict, anger, jealousy, and unhealthy competition arise in the mind, causing misery to ourselves and others. A war-like situation ensues and we begin to view others with suspicion. We presume that everyone around us is trying to pull us down. We become cynical, life seems purposeless and striving for achievement in any field seems completely pointless.

But life need not be such a conflict-ridden minefield. Life too can be played in the spirit of a game, between us and the outside world. To become champion players in life as in any other sport, we need to be well conversant with the various ideals, rules, regulations, and instruments that govern the game of life.

What Should be the Ideal for the Game of Life?

A sport may be played for many reasons. Some play just for fun. There are others who play to earn their livelihood or to earn name and fame. Popular sportsmen play for a cause in benefit shows, to help society or to collect funds or for the glory of the nation. The higher the ideal of the player, the higher is his spirit of sportsmanship.

Likewise, there are many different views about the ideals to follow in the game of life. Some say that the ideal is to eat, drink, and be merry. But what if there is no one to cook or no money to buy food or our stomach is upset? When we have a sumptuous supper laid out before us, what if some bad news interrupts our partaking of the very first morsel? So simple a desire and so complex a process of its gratification! Thus this ideal is seen to be false.

Some believe that life is meant for enjoying various luxuries and that may keep us happy all the time. We know from bitter experiences in life that seeking material pleasures does not always mean that we will be able to achieve them. Or even if we achieve everything, it is not guaranteed that we will be in a position to enjoy them. Everyday, life around us has ample evidence to suggest that the experiences of everybody's life are at best a combination of happiness and unhappiness, pleasure and pain, success and failure. It is indeed a paradox, a utopian dream to wish for perpetual happiness while pursuing material luxuries in the world.

Some people believe that the ideal of life is to earn money, name, and fame. Money helps satisfy life's many needs, but it can never be the ideal. A person may be worth billions of dollars, but if his son dies of cancer, all of it seems worthless and powerless.

Yet another view is that the ideal of life is to win at all costs. This view even approves and justifies the use of foul means to achieve the desired ends. But winning is not a true benchmark of success in life, as we have already discussed. The Indian epic, Ramayana describes how an old but brave bird Jatayu, stopped the flying chariot of Ravana who was returning to his kingdom after abducting Sita. Jatayu, the king of eagles fought Ravana with his beak and talons and wounded by the evil king, he patiently tolerated the pain and lay waiting to give the sad news to Rama. It is Jatayu, not Ravana, who is praised and extolled even today. The epic Mahabharata also depicts how the Kaurava prince Duryodhana used fraudulent means to win a gambling match against his cousin, Yudhishtira. Yet, it was Yudhishtira who was ultimately successful in life, as he held on to truth and lived a noble life. Thus, adopting dubious means and winning in life cannot be the ideal.

The only appealing and sustaining ideal in the game of life, for all times, is to live for a truthful and noble cause. The game of life has to be played in an honest and upright manner to achieve worthwhile victories in life. Only then can we derive optimum joy from all our activities.

What are the Rules and Regulations in the Game of Life?

A civil society is founded on the principle that the members of the society will formulate and accept a certain set of rules. Without this the society will soon degenerate into chaos. For instance, traffic rules ensure smooth flow of traffic and prevent accidents. A science experiment or a mathematics problem requires a set pattern of rule-based steps to obtain accurate results. Cricket, football, hockey, and for that matter every sport requires a set of rules to ensure a free and fair game. Similarly, the game of life also requires obedience to a certain set of do's and don'ts, to govern and regulate our activities. This set of rules known as dharma or righteous instructions, is prescribed by each and every religion for its followers. The scriptures warn us that a selfish and immoral life that goes against the dharma will lead to untold misery. However, one must not be good out of moral fear. We must be good because it is our nature. We must learn to outgrow the rules once we are sufficiently strong. A child must get rid of the supports if it wants to be independent.

What are the Instruments to Play the Game?

We face many difficult situations in life such as medical emergencies, loss of a loved one, failure in an exam, and so on. Just as a batsman prepares to face various types of deliveries bowled by the opposing team, we must be ready to play the game of life. A sharp intellect that can discriminate between right and wrong, determination to succeed and tremendous faith in our capacity will help us play well.

Most of us do not care to use the intellect at all and we simply concentrate on getting an education by means of filling our heads with various facts and figures. True knowledge which comes from introspection and discovery is hence ignored. As a result, the intellect and discriminating power remain stunted and are of little use. Such people find themselves stranded and completely defeated whenever some adverse situation arises. Real education must help build character and allow the growth of a more humane personality.

A parable illustrates our point beautifully. There were four friends, of whom three were educated in the various arts and sciences while the fourth, though not much educated, had an abundance of common sense. Once, while walking together through a forest, they stumbled upon a lion's carcass. The first three took this to be a good opportunity to show off their skills. The first was able to reassemble the bones and shape it into a skeleton. The second friend used his skills to put back muscle and flesh and the lion appeared to be asleep! The third friend, hoping to outdo them, was about to bring it back to life when the fourth friend cautioned them about the consequences. When his learned friends refused to listen, he asked them to wait for some time and climbed up the nearest tree. As soon as the third friend infused life into the dead lion, it killed all three of them.

This shows that mere bookish knowledge, without common sense and discrimination, is of little use and can be very harmful to the owner. Education and literacy do empower an individual, but one must also imbibe the culture to feel for others and use this power to become an enlightened citizen.

The power to discriminate between the good and bad, the right and wrong in any situation can be cultivated by developing these two faculties given to us by nature: a keen intellect to discriminate and a loving heart to feel.

11

Balance the use of the
Mind and the Intellect

'There is evil in your mind. That is why you can't find peace.'
'He who has a pure mind sees everything pure.'
—Holy Mother Sri Sarada Devi

An individual's personality is defined and determined by the quality and texture of his mind and intellect. We need to develop both in order to improve our personality. When the mind and the intellect are in order and are tuned to each other, there is harmony and rhythm in life. Else, there will be discord and harshness. Adaptability is the hallmark of a trained mind, while an untrained mind is apt to lose control when times are unfavourable.

Life is a continuous stream of experiences and an individual's quality of life depends upon the predominant nature of his experiences. While good experiences boost the will-power and self-confidence of an individual, bad experiences point out our weaknesses and strengthen our resolve to fight. The strength or weakness of a wall depend upon the quality of material used for construct- ing it. But life cannot be like the inert wall; there has to be struggle, ups, and downs. Let us not blame the mistakes that we commit; only let us not repeat them. Every human experience, be it positive or negative, involves four components—body, mind, intellect, and consciousness. Of these, the intellect or the deciding faculty is very important.

The mind is the seat of all emotions like love, ha- tred, anger, compassion, and feelings. Being happy or unhappy at any point of time depends on the state of our mind. On the other hand, the intellect is the power to discriminate, the power that allows us to determine how our mind reacts to a given situation. For instance, a certain student having failed in his exam, discrimi- nates and realizes the need to study harder. Another student in a similar situation, may vent his unhappiness in destructive ways. Some may think of suicide too. Animals too possess emotions and think, using their mind. But animals do not have the faculty of intellect and their reactions are all impulsive. Their memories too are very short when compared to humans. Humans are exceptional and using the intellect, can evolve into culturally and spiritually endowed beings. We tend to ignore this gift, especially when we are under the sway of emotions.

Raw, uncontrolled, and unrefined emotions are harmful, yet it is emotions alone that can provide us the required impetus to undertake and pursue any activity. Mere intellectual conviction without emotional support can never provide the energy that is needed to forge ahead on any path. This is the reason why some people, otherwise very bright and intelligent are not able to make much progress in their careers. They lack passion or emotional love for their work and career advancement.

To refine the intellect, one needs to control the senses and the mind. Emotions should be directed to a higher channel of creativity, a higher purpose. Man has a creative urge and that can be satisfied by engaging oneself in music, literature, arts, or gardening, thereby refining the emotions and expressing them at a higher level. The purpose of refining the emotions is to realize our true nature by getting rid of the idea that we are limited to the body. We need to train ourselves to use the intellect as a tool to channel our emotions. Emotions can misguide us. But the practice of introspection helps in controlling both, intellect and emotions.

The story of a blind man and a lame man who used their respective strengths to cross a busy road, illustrates how the mind and the intellect can be tuned to achieve best results. In this story, the blind man is physically strong and can run across the road but is unable to see his way through the maze of passing vehicles. The lame man is intelligent enough to make judgements about the passing traffic, but cannot quickly make his way across the road. In order to overcome their respective weaknesses, the blind man carries the lame one on his shoulder. The arrangement helps the former navigate through the traffic, fully confident of the directions and judgement made by the latter. The blind man represents the mind and the lame man represents the intellect. Taking a cue, we should likewise submit all the inputs of our mind to the intellect.

To balance our mind and intellect, we consciously need to stop the misuse of our eyes and ears. The mind is adversely affected when we indulge in gossip, watch movies or television, frequent fashionable joints, and so on. Such a distracted mind is ever ready to fall a prey to all sorts of temptations and thus invites immense sorrow. The eyes and ears are particularly responsible for distracting the mind. We must try to see and hear only that which benefits our inner selves. A license given to senses weakens the mind and saps the body of its vigour.

Compare the mind to an office clerk and the mind's inputs to the incoming letters. The receiving clerk has been instructed by his superior to only receive incoming letters and pass them up the hierarchy for necessary action. If the clerk starts opening the letters on his own and passes orders, without referring them to the designated higher official, chaos will ensue. Similarly, if the mind, under the control of various emotions, dances to the tune of the sensory inputs without passing them for scrutiny to the intellect, life will be ruined.

Thoughts arising in the mind through the sense inputs are like the flow of water in a river. The intellect is like the river's embankments. When the river's banks are solid and firm, the water force remains directed and controlled and it flows smoothly and powerfully. When there is a breach, the water overflows, causing floods and devastation. Similarly, as long as our discriminating power is strong, our thoughts remain focused and controlled, giving us the strength to achieve greater heights in our respective pursuits.

We behave intelligently, rationally, and have a balanced approach towards life only when the intellect takes appropriate decisions based on the inputs provided by the mind. The intellect is the best judge to decide as to when and in what circumstances our mind should entertain or reject a particular input or thought. The *Katha* Upanishad compares the body to a chariot. The horses are the senses, the mind the reins and the intellect is the charioteer, who works according to the instructions of the rider, the Self. If the horses are well broken, reins strong and kept well in the hands of the charioteer, then the goal is easily attained. If not, destruction is certain. The purpose of the chariot or the body is to function according to the rider's wishes. The Self is the rider and all our faculties are functioning due to its association with the body. The moment the Self leaves the body, we become inert matter. So, the mind and intellect must function in unison to please the Self, which is ever pure, blissful, and all-knowing.

12
Control Your Anger

At one time, Holy Mother's niece, Radhu was pestering
her for some favour. Since Mother did not have the required
money to fulfil her desire, she refused and Radhu, becoming
furious, struck the Mother in the back with an eggplant. As
the vegetable struck her, Mother bent her back in pain and
the place became red and swollen. But unmindful of this, she
turned to the Master and said with folded hands, 'Master
don't be offended by her; she is ignorant.' So great was the
Mother's forbearance!

—Gospel of Holy Mother

An old precept says that anger is a great sin. The Bhagavad Gita also says that anger leads to clouded thinking and finally to destruction. We are aware that anger hurts us and the society. When left to escalate, anger of an individual or a community can cause war, family break-ups and senseless murders. In most cases, the resultant destruction could have been avoided—if only the people involved could have somehow curbed their anger and tried to solve matters calmly and amicably. Even in our own lives, we find many occasions when anger has caused us trouble: quarrels within the family, unpopularity at the office, loss of friends—the list is long! Obviously, it is of paramount importance then that we learn to control our anger and channel our energies in a more productive way.

Anger may be defined as an emotion or a feeling or as the expression of emotion. Anger can also be a form of concentrated lust. We get angry when our desires are not fulfilled. Earlier, while categorizing the causes of human suffering, three broad categories were identified—conflict between man and nature, between man and other living beings, and within one's own mind.

Whatever the source, the effects of anger can be very negative and destructive. It is a sheer waste of energy. Medical science has proven that anger can cause heartburn, ulcers, blood pressure, and heart trouble. The Mahabharata wisely cautions us—'An angry person commits mistakes that lead to his own destruction.' This can be demonstrated by these instances.

A certain family in a village had a mongoose as a pet. It was loved and trusted like a family member. Once, the woman of the house had to go out to fetch water and she entrusted her little baby to the care of her pet. The alert mongoose detected a snake sneaking into the house, and recognizing the threat to the baby, jumped on it at once and killed it. In the process, its mouth was covered with blood. When the mother returned, the mongoose ran joyfully towards her, expecting to be appreciated for its efforts. Seeing blood on its face, she imagined that the pet had harmed her baby and in a fit of anger, picked up a stone and killed the mongoose on the spot! Only later did she realize her grave mistake when she saw the snake lying dead near the cradle of her blissfully asleep infant. Under the influence of anger a person loses the power to discriminate between right and wrong!

An angry person vents out his anger by uttering all kinds of menacing expressions like, 'I will kill you', 'I will break his head', and so on. Such utterances only worsen the situation and lead to further escalation of anger and violence.

Once, Hanuman was possessed by anger. He mistook some white flowers to be red. Those who were with him pointed out the mistake. But, unwilling to accept defeat, he insisted that those particular flowers were red until Sri Rama made him realize that anger had distorted his perception. Anger can make things appear as different from what they actually are. In a fit of anger we see people as more evil and obnoxious than they really are. Doing so, we react in ways that may cause more harm. For instance, consider how a husband shouts at his wife in a fit of anger. And yet, only a few minutes ago, he was professing undying love for her! Goaded by anger, he even goes to the extent of demanding an immediate divorce!

Anger can unsettle the mind of even a great sage. Once, Sri Ramakrishna asked Rakhal, one of his direct disciples, to prepare a betel roll for him. Rakhal refused saying that he had neither done such a thing earlier nor knew how to do it. Latu, another direct disciple who was also present, was incensed at this disobedience to the Guru. He started shouting at Rakhal, who calmly bore those insults. At this Sri Ramakrishna smiled and said that since Rakhal had perfect control on his anger, he was the better disciple, even though he had disobeyed his Guru. When a relationship becomes strained or when there is turmoil within a family, its cause can be traced to anger. Anger born of frustration is even more dangerous and is often unreasonable.

We must declare anger our greatest enemy and defeat it. Only weak persons shout to defend themselves. The strong willed are calm and radiate power in demanding situations. To enjoy a happy and peaceful life, we must learn how to conquer anger.

Our primary tool against anger management is the intellect, which can be used to control emotions. This aspect has been discussed in detail in the preceding chapter. Animals do not have this tool and therefore lack self-control. Even the slightest provocation sparks off a fierce defensive reaction in them. Unfortunately, we humans do not use our intellect adequately and at times behave like animals. Emotions, when checked and controlled by the intellect become a positive force to reckon with.

Anger is directly proportional to desire. When desire is strong, anger gains intensity. A teenager, keen on spending the evening with his friends, becomes angry when his father assigns him some household chores. If his father had interrupted him when he was about to go to the market to fetch milk, he would be relatively less angry. His desire to visit the friend's house is stronger than the desire to help his parents because his priorities are different. If he had always been obedient and loving to his parents then he would not have refused their request.

Bhagavan Buddha was begging alms and the owner of a house started hurling abuses at him. The Buddha heard him calmly and asked, 'Sir, if you gift something to someone and he refuses to accept it, then to whom does the gift belong?' The man replied, 'Why, it belongs to the person who gave the gift.' The Buddha smiled and said, 'I have not accepted the words that you just gifted me!' Dr. Samuel Johnson was one of the greatest literary figures of England and the compiler of the first comprehensive English dictionary. A certain Mr. Boswell approached Dr. Johnson for counsel over some insult heaped upon him by someone. His temper was calmed by Dr. Johnson's words—'Today's insult will become insignificant after one year.' This shows that when our passions subside, the intensity reduces. If we take a few moments to introspect and analyse our anger, we will have practised effective anger control.

The following scale is a means to measure the level that we have attained in controlling anger and also the depth of anger: Anger lasts for a few seconds in noble people, for two hours in the mediocre and for a full day in the lower class. In wicked persons however, anger lasts till death. To which category would we like to belong? Here are a few tips that help control anger.

Practise Waiting for Five Minutes Before Reacting in a fit of Anger

At the end of five minutes, we may find that our anger is unjustified. We may have wanted to shout and scream, but on after-thought it becomes clear that only a few words will suffice!

Simply Leave the Place if the Surroundings are not Conducive to Anger Control

Sometimes flight is better than fight. A change in the environment can change our outlook, bringing in its wake some amount of calmness. For example, if someone irritates you at home, try taking a walk outside for a few minutes. In most cases, you will find that your mind is clear by the time you return.

Stand Before a Mirror and Examine the Expressions That Appear on Your Face in a fit of Anger

The flushed face and excessive sweat of an angry person will point out that he is not presentable and appealing. Anger robs one of normal composure and he starts projecting a disgusting personality.

Think About the Damage Caused by Anger Before Expressing it

Reason, analyse and know that you will lose, not gain anything by being angry. The immense damage that it causes to your relationship with your dear ones should be sufficient warning.

Convince Yourself Again and Again that the World Cannot Move as per Your Wishes

We labour under the misconception that the world is designed to suit our purposes and that we are very important. When we find things going against our wishes, we get annoyed. If we reduce our ego and realize that the world waits for none, our demands and expectations will also reduce and we shall be less irritated by adverse events.

In addition to these simple techniques, there are two more subtle but very effective techniques that can be used to control anger.

Practise Concentration When You are Angry

Suppose you are angry with me. Now try to observe the condition of your mind carefully. First my face and then my whole body appears in your mind. Then, suddenly, the intense feeling called anger arises in your mind. I am the object against which your anger is flowing. Anger melts away if you can distance it from the object of anger. The trick is to separate the object and the feeling for that object. It may require a little practice initially, but is worth trying, as this is one of the most effective techniques. Using this technique, you can conquer any passion.

Stop Pre-supposing About the Person You are Cross With

Suppose you are angry with, say, Mr. Ram Babu. You then start guessing and imagining various things about Mr. Ram Babu. 'He misbehaves like that always, I know him very well from the beginning. I knew that he will act this way. I should not encourage him by overlooking his faults. He should be punished. I have my faults. But his faults are more than mine. I will say something directly or indirectly...' Actually, we are concentrating our thoughts on that person and this stimulates and strengthens the feeling of anger. The more you imagine, the more powerful will be your anger. Try to counter anger by forcibly bringing in thoughts of love, your previous happy moments with him, and the help that you have received from him, and anger will subside. This is called 'pratipaksha bhavana' in the Yoga scriptures.

Sometimes, anger may be justified. For instance, parents may scold and even slap their beloved child when repeated requests and warnings fail to prevent him from playing with fire. This show of anger is constructive as it is used for a good purpose. Such anger is under our control, whereas, destructive form of anger controls us. It is the latter that we have to avoid. It is important to note that we need to remain aware, alert and pay attention to even a slight hint of anger erupting within our mind. Mostly we tend to fire as soon as the spark arises! But this has to be controlled through practice. We must learn not to react on the spur of the moment. There must be a gap between the impulse of anger and the expression of anger. Otherwise, there is no hope of controlling anger.

A few use their intellect and break out of the bondage of this action-reaction mechanism. It is this set of people who can claim to be true humans and who are worthy of respect and emulation. It is only by practising control of our mind through the intellect that we can be more humane, less animal-like and thus able to develop better values in life. The various steps in developing higher values are—control of mind, assimilation of right ideas, creation of higher values, and continuous effort towards achieving the higher goal. The cultivation of such desired traits in our personalities can be effectively achieved through the practice of *Satsanga*, Discipline and Meditation (SDM). Through SDM, love for God will gradually increase and evil passions such as jealousy, anger, selfishness, and so on will gradually drop away. Sri Ramakrishna has said that as one approaches closer and closer to God, one's passions and ego become more and more distant. When we start walking towards the North, South will move away automatically.

Swami Vivekananda has said that we waste two-thirds of our energy in useless emotions such as anger. Even people who have reached the pinnacle of their respective careers—be they renowned doctors, great scientists, or accomplished musicians, use at the most only one-third of their energies. Through control of anger, one gradually learns to tap the remaining two-thirds of energy stored within. Just imagine all that we could achieve if we had access to even a fraction of the remaining two-thirds of our energy. All our dreams and projects would then be within our reach!

13
Curb Your Jealousy

"Avoid jealousy and selfishness. Be obedient and eternally faithful to the cause of truth, humanity, and your country, and you will move the world."

—Swami Vivekananda

Jealousy, like anger or greed, is another emotion that springs from our survival instinct—the struggle to be better than others so that one can compete better. It can arise from an inferiority complex also, a state of mind where the person somehow resents the superiority of others. The cause of jealousy is the desire for self-importance, especially in comparison with others. An individual starts feeling jealous when he suffers from a sense of worthlessness and wishes to be 'somebody' in order to gain recognition. For instance, when a student of the class stands first in the annual exams, some of his classmates become jealous of him. It is because they too desire the position and respect that he enjoys. It is the same in every field of human endeavour. When jealous, we waste time deprecating others rather than appreciating their hard work or emulating their virtues. It is better to delve on one's own achievements and build on them rather than feel sorry about another's progress.

Jealousy is one of the greatest enemies of happiness. Jealousy is caused by cut-throat competition, modern-day stress, and the negative influences of a fast life that are widespread in workplaces, homes, schools or colleges. There are some who cannot bear to see their co-workers being praised by the boss, while there are others who have difficulty in accepting the reality of their competitor getting more business. There are those who cannot bear to see their own relatives doing well, like the woman who got terribly upset upon knowing that her husband's nephew gained admission to a reputed medical college while her own son failed to clear the entrance exams. She went about telling her neighbours that the medical profession had become degraded and therefore no talented child would aspire any longer to pursue a career in medicine! Such people achieve little peace in life as petty hatred keeps them preoccupied.

Perverse are the ways of jealousy. A jealous person finds joy if his enemy is in trouble and feels sad when he sees him prosper. Others' suffering evoke sympathy in the normal individual, but not so in the jealous. Swami Vivekananda has said, 'Jealousy is a terrible, horrible sin.'

A jealous person is never at ease. He or she is in constant discomfort, is ever discontented and can never appreciate the good qualities of others. Such persons are always on the lookout for faults in whoever happens to be the object of their jealousy. When they are unable to find faults, they don't mind using deceit and improper means to ruin their enemy's reputation. Once, there were two ascetics practicing austerities to please God. Pleased by their devotion, God appeared separately before each of them, to grant boons. The first ascetic humbly said that he would be happy with twice of whatever was bestowed to the other. God, wanting to watch the fun, informed the second ascetic about the peculiar request of the first. Not wanting to see him better, the second ascetic pleaded for blindness in one eye! Not being satisfied with this, the now one-eyed man dug a pit in front of the blind man's hut, so that the latter would fall in and get killed. Such is the impact of jealousy that even after beholding God they could not forgive and forget. Jealousy can turn the heads of even good and virtuous people.

Jealousy is found even in children and is called sibling rivalry. If the mother loves or favours a child, the other gets jealous and impatient. To avoid such situations, parents should be impartial, and must not pamper their children with gifts and undue appreciation.

To get rid of jealousy, we must first accept that it is a mental disease and take steps to cure it. We cannot continue to afford wasting energy in hating others. The following simple tips can help curb jealousy.

Do Not Give Anyone the Keys to Your Happiness

The moment we start hating someone out of jealousy, we automatically give him or her, the right to exercise control over our sleep, hunger, blood pressure and happiness. Moreover, due to jealousy we are unable to digest the food that we eat. Nor are we able to sleep peacefully. Happiness is lost and life becomes full of stress. But, if we introspect, does feeling jealous help us in any way? No. Our jealousy cannot stop another's progress. Instead, it ruins our peace and we burn in hatred. It distracts us and does not allow us to make the required dedicated effort to achieve our own goals. In short, jealousy throws a spanner in the works of our own progress.

Stop Making Prejudiced and Negative Comparisons With Others

Feelings of jealousy appear in the mind when we compare ourselves with others and believe that our achievements are inferior to theirs. We then start fearing and disliking others and such prejudiced comparisons prevent us from appreciating and learning from their good qualities. In fact, jealousy can also pervert our mind to such an extent that we start seeing ourselves as superior to others—simply because we cannot bear accepting that someone else can be better than us.

We must introspect, analyse, and accept reality. As mentioned earlier in this book, each one of us, irrespective of caste, creed, or nationality is a 'child of immortality', with infinite potential within. Each person has his own place in society and each is great in his own place. Why do we need to pose as 'somebody' and indulge in kite-flying imagination? Doing our assigned duties to the best of our capacity and progressing individually and collectively with the society must be our aim in life. All else will fail to matter if we end up neglecting this aim. Comparing ourselves with others to emulate their example is healthy. To feel envious and deride their achievements is meanness.

If at all we need to compare, let us compare with our own achievements. Let us see where we were a month ago and where we stand today. Such comparison will be beneficial both in controlling jealousy and in motivating us further, so that we can strive harder to achieve our goals.

Learn to Appreciate That Other People can Also be Good and Important

Most of us cannot tolerate if somebody is being praised. Our ears desire self-praise, for it boosts our ego. And no sooner do we hear people praising someone else, we retort by saying, 'What is so special about him? Why do you praise him so? I have heard the opposite of what you are saying about him', and so on.

By saying so, we belittle ourselves. Slowly we will lose credibility and our opinions will never be considered seriously anymore.

Learn to be Content With What you Have

One must learn to be content with whatever life provides him. We get what we deserve. If we need more material possessions and better comforts, we need to work hard to possess them in the 'right' way. Contentment is a virtue one needs to practise. What we do not deserve will not stay with us, even if we try to possess it by hook or by crook.

It is no use worrying about the privileges and material comforts owned by other people. There can never be equal distribution of all things in nature. If that were to happen, life will become monotonous and all variety would be lost. We will become like robots, all similar and expressing the same emotions! Variety is the spice of life. Just as we have variety in languages, dress, and culture, there has to be variety in living conditions too. Nature abhors uniformity.

This however does not mean that the wealthy are entitled to have more. There are a number of laws to ensure that each person is cared for. Social structure does not allow hoarding. Sooner or later power and wealth get distributed. Fortunes keep shifting. It is only when we start envying others that we feel deprived. Great men take pride in the richness of their personality rather than their possessions.

The quotation from Swami Vivekananda that was used while discussing the chapter, 'Learn the Art of Action' is worth repeating here. 'What you have earned by your past actions none can take away from you. If you have deserved wealth, you can bury yourself in the forest and it will come to you. If you have deserved good food and clothing, you may go to the North Pole and they will be brought to you. The polar bear will bring them. If you have not deserved them, you may conquer the world and will die of starvation.'

Balance the use of the Mind and Intellect

Jealousy overpowers the mind and the intellect, and therefore we cannot discriminate between the real and the imaginary. And as in anger, jealousy too makes us see objects not as they actually are, but as our mind likes them to appear, which is, a distorted version of reality. We therefore need to balance the use of our mind and intellect in order to overcome negative emotions like anger and jealousy.

Practise Concentration When you are Jealous

Whenever the feeling of jealousy arises in your mind, try to observe carefully the condition of your mind. First the person's face and then his whole body appears in your mind. Then suddenly the intense feeling called jealousy arises in your mind. The feeling of jealousy is distinct from the object. Learn to focus not on the object, but on the feeling. By concentrating on the feeling and not on the object, we will find that jealousy slowly melts away. Try to counter jealousy with thoughts of love, admiration, kindness, and so on. The positive forces will nullify the negative. The same trick was prescribed to get rid of anger too.

Take Action Before Nature's Blows Make you Mend Your Ways

It is important to realize that unless we voluntarily change, nature will force its methods to cure us. Nature gives us several blows so that we accept the truth and follow the right path. It is like the police treating a die-hard criminal in their custody. If simple methods like questioning and threatening do not work, the police repeatedly use physical and mental torture, until the culprit yields and speaks out the truth.

Nature plays the role of the police at times. Nature will keep giving blows in the form of tension, stress, and so on and we are forced to change our ways. The moment we start hating someone, we fail to perceive reality as it truly exists, and accept a distorted version that is projected by our mind. As the degree of jealousy increases, the degree of suffering also increases. Perhaps, after weeks or months or years, when such torture becomes unbearable, the time comes when we are ultimately forced to accept the truth that he or she may be better in some aspects while we are better in something else. All of us are born different and have different tendencies. We have to progress in our own

line like the runner who cannot change his track to
get to the first position.

Practise Introspection

We require regular practice of introspection to see
if there is any feeling of jealousy within our mind and
also to guard ourselves against its evil effects.

One very effective method for controlling not only
jealousy but all other passions is to practise *Satsanga*,
Discipline and Meditation—or SDM—as explained in
the appendix.

Practise! Practise! Practise!

Weeding out all kinds of negativity like anger, jealousy, greed, and so on must be a compulsion for us if
we sincerely wish to change for the better. We suffer
because we remain complacent and do not give due
importance to the fundamental problems plaguing us.
And even when these are brought to our notice, we are
too casual in our approach and do not follow the advice
given to us. We treat it as optional and say, 'There is a
full life before me, why hurry? Let me enjoy and live
life. Later in life when I have time and resources, I
will cure myself of all the ills...' Our entire life is worn
out in this manner and we fail to inculcate the desired
self-discipline.

The ego also prevents us from accepting the fact
that we have defects in us. It is good to have a healthy
ego which gives us our individuality, but harmful to

have egotism—the tendency to feel superior to others. Sri Ramakrishna would distinguish between ripe ego and unripe ego. Ripe ego is born of maturity, whereas unripe ego is selfish.

The struggle to reach perfection is demanding and one needs to be constantly on the alert. 'It is like walking on the edge of a sharp razor', says the *Katha* Upanishad. Perseverance and dedicated effort alone can give results. Swami Vivekananda has captured this thought in a beautiful quotation, 'The whole day mixing with the world with *Karma Kanda* (worldly duties), and in the evening sitting down and blowing through your nose! Is it so easy? Should *Rishis* come flying through the air, because you have blown three times through the nose? Is it a joke? It is all nonsense. What is needed is *Chittashuddhi*, purification of the heart.' If we really wish to improve, we must purify ourselves by weeding out dangerous passions like anger and jealousy. This kind of control and purity must manifest itself at all times in our lives. In fact, while talking to one of his disciples, Swamiji says that even in our dreams there must be no hint of impurity! This purification of the heart and the strength to control anger and jealousy can be acquired through SDM.

We must start practicing the methods required to cleanse our mind right now. We must try to undo all our evil habits. A ten-year old child, reading a medical book will not become a doctor overnight. Similarly, reading self-improvement material or scriptures will not help if we do not will to change and practice. The holy texts such as the Gita or the Upanishads can give us the directions but the walking has to be done by us, slowly and steadily. Swami Vivekananda has said 'Arise, awake and stop not till the goal is reached.' Let us draw inspiration from all such sources, keep our hearts open to their ennobling influences, allow our mind to ponder on these ideas, and follow in their footsteps to achieve the goal of our lives.

Part III

Appendix

14
What is SDM?

S: *Satsanga* means holy company. The environment and the company that we keep influence the mind to a great extent. One can realize this fact by analysing the condition of the mind when one visits a holy place like a temple and when one visits a film theatre or a fashionable place like New Delhi's Connaught Place or Mumbai's Bandstand. The word '*Satsanga*' means a favourable environment that helps elevate the mind, to a higher level from the lower level of worldly thought. *Satsanga* can be of various types: being in the presence of holy people, attending spiritual classes, reading uplifting books, listening to good music, and *bhajans*, and so on. One should devote some time everyday for *Satsanga*. In the initial stages, *Satsanga* is indispensable. But instead of depending on the external input always, we must be able to get this *Satsanga* from the Atman, our true nature and our constant companion.

D: Disciplined life or doing everything systematically and with active interest is vital to life management. Discipline helps by restraining us from unplanned actions. Since we become conscious of time, reactions to unwanted impulses are reduced. A student achieves academic success when he strictly adheres to the time-table of the school or college. A man of business cannot delay in serving his customers or in getting fresh stock. So, discipline inculcates a sense of punctuality and responsibility. One should make a timetable of his daily activities and try to follow it. This will prevent him from postponing important tasks and incurring damage. The art of time management is essential to success in all fields. A moment's delay can ruin a person and an opportunity lost is gone forever.

M: Meditation or watching the thought flow is essential to life management because, thoughts make the man. Thoughts continually arise in the mind like the waves in an ocean. Some thoughts absorb us while others are not of much consequence. Each thought will further carry the impulse to act. Therefore it is essential to control and check unnecessary thoughts from occupying our mind. Unwanted thoughts can drain psychic energy and increase the stress in an individual.

There is a big difference between brooding over thoughts and watching thoughts. We brood because we identify with the thought and at that moment forget all else. Watching is possible only when we see our thoughts without attachment. For example, we can watch and count the patches of white clouds moving in the sky. But the counting stops when we get attached to a specific white cloud and start brooding on it—Oh!

The shape of the cloud reminds me of a friend's face or my pet dog or a favorite sweetmeat. How not to get attached to thoughts? Here is an example. It is like a person surfing television channels to see what is being aired, without any intention of watching and without getting tempted to view a particular channel. This is one method of watching one's own thoughts in a disengaged way, as a mute witness. Yet another example is that of a watchman at a gate, watching people go in and out. He impartially watches them until he sees his wife enter and starts talking to her. He gets caught in the conversation and forgets to watch others getting in!

One should practice watching the thought flow daily, for at least ten minutes in the morning and evening. This is to be done in a sitting posture with the backbone held straight and eyes closed. Preferably, the legs should also be in a crossed position. Sit in that position and breathing slowly, watch the thoughts go past, without reacting to them or in other words, without brooding on them. Once this practice is established, the time can be gradually increased. This has been further explained in the next chapter.

15
Watching the Thought Flow

How to Practice it Successfully

1. The primary requirement for successful 'Watching the Thought Flow' exercise is correct body posture.

2. You need to sit cross-legged, straight, with shoulders upright; the spinal cord, back of the neck and head held in one straight line; without any backrest or hand-rest. The body should be relaxed and your hands should be placed softly on the lap.

3. For the first few minutes, you should focus on bringing the mind to that place and visualise yourself as relaxed and perfectly still.

4. You should not move any part of the body apart from breathing gently and rhythmically through the nose.

5. Once your body is absolutely still and completely relaxed, you can start 'Watching your Thoughts'.

6. Now, you must simply watch the thoughts as they appear in the mind—just as we watch clouds float by in the sky or waves come and go at the seashore.

7. It is important that you do not react to any thought; otherwise you will get lost in it and will start brooding on your thoughts, instead of watching them.

8. Try to focus on yourself, the observer who is watching all these thoughts. Look at yourself as separate from your thoughts, as the pure, eternal Self or Atman that is beyond death and decay. The light of the Self illuminates all thoughts and perceptions. Try to identify your ego with the Self and tell yourself that you are not the body or the mind.

9. Initially, one may find that the thoughts appearing in the mind are very foul and dirty. But you must not lose heart and should go on with the practice. When you wash an inkpot, only blue water keeps coming out. But as you persist in the washing process, gradually the water becomes clearer and clearer until it is absolutely pure. Similarly, you must patiently cleanse the mind with good thoughts, God's name, incidents from the lives of saints and you will find that gradually your thoughts are becoming purer and purer. Prayer to God is a great help in cleansing the mind of all worldly dross and worries.

10. The essential thing is regularity and sincerity. Be true to yourself. The practice must be done for at least ten minutes every morning and evening.

16
Inspiring Words from
The Holy Mother

Everyone can break down something, but how many can build it up?

Man finds faults in others after bringing down his own mind to that level. Does anything ever happen to another if you enumerate his faults? It only injures you. This has been my attitude. Hence I cannot see anybody's faults. If a man does a trifle for me, I try to remember him even for that. To see the faults of others! One should never do it. I never do so. Forgiveness is Tapasya.

As long as a man has desires there is no end to his transmigration. It is the desires alone that make him take one body after another. There will be rebirth for a man if he has even the desire to eat a piece of candy... Desire may be compared to a minute seed. It is like a big banyan tree growing out of a seed, which is no bigger than a dot. Rebirth is inevitable so long as one has desires. It is like taking the soul from one pillowcase and putting it into another. Only one or two out of many men can be found who are free from all desires.

Be sincere in your practice, words and deeds. You will feel blessed! His blessings are always showered on all creatures on the earth. It is needless to ask for it. Practise meditation sincerely and you will understand His infinite grace. God wants sincerity, truthfulness, and love. Outward verbal effusions do not touch Him.

The whole world is a dream; even this (the waking state) is a dream...What you dreamt last night does not exist now... A farmer who had lost a son dreamt at night that he was a king and the father of eight sons. When the dream had vanished, he said to his wife, 'Shall I weep for my eight sons or this one?'

The happiness of the world is transitory. The less you become attached to the world, the more you enjoy peace of mind.

Everything depends on one's mind. Nothing can be achieved without purity of mind. It is said, 'The aspirant may have received the grace of the Guru, the Lord and the Vaishnava; but he comes to grief without the grace of the 'one' '. That 'one' is the mind. The mind of the aspirant should be gracious to him.

in the evening. That acts as a rudder to a boat. When one sits in meditation in the evening, one gets a chance to think of what one has done—good or bad—during the whole day. Next, one should compare the state of one's mind on the previous day with the present. ... Unless you meditate in the mornings and evenings along with work, how can you know what you are actually doing?

Mother: You have rolled different threads on a reel—red, black and white. While unrolling you will see them all exactly in the same way.

Disciple: How many insignificant desires crop up in our mind! How can we get rid of them?

Mother: In your case these are no real desires. They are nothing. They are mere fancies that appear and disappear in your mind. The more they come and go, the better for you... So long as the ego exists, desires also undoubtedly remain. But those desires will not injure you.

Whenever people discuss good or evil, all those who are present have to take a little share of the good or evil... Suppose someone tells you about his good and evil deeds. Everytime you think of that person you must perforce remember his good and evil deeds. In this manner his good and evil deeds both must leave some impression upon your mind.

How can one's mind be healthy if one doesn't work? No one can spend all twenty-four hours in thought and meditation. So one must engage oneself in work; it keeps the mind cheerful.

The mind keeps well when engaged in work. And yet Japa, meditation, prayer also are specially needed. You must at least sit down once in the morning and again

My child, this mind is just like a wild elephant. It races with the wind. Therefore one should discriminate all the time. One should work hard for the realization of God.

Disciple: I cannot concentrate my mind well during meditation. My mind is fickle and unsteady.

Mother: Don't worry! Restlessness is the nature of the mind, as it is of the eyes and ears. Practise regularly. The Name of God is more powerful than the senses. Always think of the Master, who is looking after you. Don't be troubled about your lapses.

If you practise spiritual discipline for sometime in a solitary place, you will find that your mind has become strong and then you can live in any place or society without being in the least affected by it. When the plant is tender it should be hedged around. But when it has grown big, cows, and goats cannot injure it.

Regarding weakness of the mind, Holy Mother said to a disciple, 'Child, this is the law of nature. Have you not noticed the full moon and the new moon? Likewise the mind is sometimes dominated by good and sometimes by bad tendencies.'

Disciple: I have been practicing religious disciplines. I do not relax my efforts in that direction. But it appears that the impurities of mind are not reducing.